THE FOUNTAINWELL DRAMA TEXTS

General Editors

T. A. DUNN

ANDREW GURR

JOHN HORDEN

A. NORMAN JEFFARES

R. L. C. LORIMER

Assistant General Editor

BRIAN W. M. SCOBIE

7

JOHN MARSTON

THE
DUTCH COURTESAN

Edited by
PETER DAVISON

OLIVER & BOYD

EDINBURGH

1968

OLIVER AND BOYD LTD
Tweeddale Court
Edinburgh 1

First Published   1968

Hardback 05 001567 2
Paperback 05 001684 9

Printed in Great Britain by
T. & A. CONSTABLE LTD, Hopetoun Street
Edinburgh

ACKNOWLEDGMENTS

This edition was begun in Sydney, Australia, in 1961 as one of a series I was then trying to launch for use by students of that university. I should first, therefore, like to express my gratitude to the Fisher Library of the University of Sydney for obtaining microfilms for me and for allowing me to retain them on my return to England until the task of editing was completed. I am also grateful to The Shakespeare Institute, University of Birmingham, for obtaining a microfilm for me and for making its facilities available to me; and to the British Museum, and Victoria and Albert Museum, to the Library of Congress, the Boston Public Library, and the Pforzheimer, Harvard, Chapin, Folger, Huntingdon, and Bodleian Libraries for making microfilms available. The Dyce Librarian was kind enough to make a special search on my behalf.

Every editor owes general debts of gratitude to his predecessors and to those who have evolved bibliographic techniques; these I gratefully acknowledge. In this context I would particularly mention the most recent editor of *The Dutch Courtesan*, Dr Martin Wine, often though I have found myself in disagreement with his readings and interpretations. Specific acknowledgments to Dr Wine and earlier editors are made within the edition.

I am also grateful to the General Editors of this series, to Professor A. N. Jeffares and Professor T. A. Dunn for many helpful comments, and to the late Professor K. G. W. Cross for help that goes back to our days at the University of Sydney.

Finally, Mistress Mulligrub's reply to her husband's plea at II. III. 112 virtually demands that I dedicate this edition to my eldest son, Simon.

P. H. D.

Birmingham
December, 1966

CONTENTS

CRITICAL INTRODUCTION

It is surprising that *The Dutch Courtesan* has not made a greater appeal to modern audiences and producers than has, in fact, been the case. It was performed in London in 1954 and 1959 by Joan Littlewood's Theatre Workshop and by the National Theatre in 1964 in a production directed by William Gaskell and Piers Haggard; at the time of writing it has achieved a brief "Off Off-Broadway" production in New York at the Casa Italiana Renaissance Theater.[1] The success of the National Theatre production was greater, perhaps, than many critics allowed, but that "Off Off-Broadway" presentation, beyond the fringe of regular theatrical productions, accurately places *The Dutch Courtesan* in terms of actual performance since Marston's death. The theatrical merits of the play, and especially of its sub-plot, have been recognised since the Restoration, at least to the extent that Marston's play has proved a fruitful quarry for pillaging and adaptation.[2] Why is it, then, that the play as a whole should have proved less artistically and commercially viable in the theatre than its characteristics might lead one to expect? Does the reason lie in the nature of contemporary theatre and its audiences; is there, perhaps, too little common ground between Marston and an audience not of his own time; or is there a flaw in the play itself?

The original audience for *The Dutch Courtesan* lived in the very first years of the reign of James VI and I. The play must have been written between 1603 (for it draws from Florio's translation of Montaigne's *Essays*, published in that year) and 1605, when it appeared in print with, on its title page, the statement that it had been performed at the Blackfriars by the Children of Her Majesty's Revels. (Her Majesty was Anne of Denmark, wife of James I.) Chambers proposed 1603-4,[3]

---

[1] *The Village Voice*, New York, 30 June 1966, p. 16.

[2] See J. J. Elson, *The Wits* (1932); and Leo Hughes and Arthur H. Scouten, "Some Theatrical Adaptations of a Picaresque Tale", in *Studies in English*, XXVI (1945–6), pp. 98–114.

[3] E. K. Chambers, *The Elizabethan Stage* (1923) III, 430. K. G. W. Cross has also proposed 1603 for *The Dutch Courtesan*; see "The Date of *The Malcontent* Once More", in *P.Q.*, XXXIX (1960), p. 108.

a date Wine considers to be likely,[4] but Caputi has argued very strongly for Marston's play succeeding, or at least being composed simultaneously with, *Eastward Ho!*[5] He endeavours to show that Marston "derived much of his technique" for *The Dutch Courtesan* (in particular the construction of a plot based on broad contrasts in character) from working with Jonson and Chapman on *Eastward Ho!* and that it was from this particular association with Jonson that he derived the economic value-system commonly to be found in Jonson's plays.

That Marston was influenced by Jonson in this respect is not unlikely, but this is not the dominant feature of *The Dutch Courtesan*, and it need not have been due to working on *Eastward Ho!* As Caputi says himself, the use of plots involving contrasts in character was common in Marston's time and Marston may have become aware of the dramatic possibilities of the economic value-system from plays written before *Eastward Ho!*[6]

Apart from the possible influence of Jonson, the play is derived from three kinds of source—prose fiction, the drama of the period, and Montaigne's *Essays*. The main story is taken from *Les Bergeries de Juliette* by Nicolas de Montreulx.[7] Part of the sub-plot is drawn from Painter's *Palace of Pleasure* and some from clown acts of earlier drama.[8] Dramatic tradition is doubtless also responsible for the Beatrice-Benedict-like relationship of Crispinella and Tysefew, for the comic Watch, the shaving of Mulligrub, and his being tormented in the stocks, and for the bawdy Nurse (the similarity to Shakespeare's Nurse being obvious). Marston's indebtedness to the recent drama of his time for so many aspects of *The Dutch Courtesan* suggests that he was keenly aware of what was current in the theatre, and it is thus the less probable that the technique of contrasting characterisation and the dramatic potentialities of the economic value-system are due

---

[4] Marston, *The Dutch Courtesan*, ed. M. L. Wine (1965). All references to Wine are to this edition, hereafter cited as *Wine*.

[5] Anthony Caputi, *John Marston, Satirist* (1961) pp. 219 f, hereafter cited as *Caputi*.

[6] Caputi's interpretation of other evidence, such as the failure to use on the title page the formula "as it hath been sundry times played" is interesting but not, I think, convincing.

[7] John J. O'Connor, "The Chief Source of Marston's *Dutch Courtesan*", in *S.P.*, LIV, pp. 509–15. See also *Wine*, xiv–xv.

[8] James J. Jackson, "Sources of the Subplot of Marston's *The Dutch Courtesan*", in *P.Q.*, XXXI, p. 223 f.

to his association with Jonson in the composition of *Eastward Ho!* as Caputi suggests.

The importance of the third influence, Montaigne's *Essays*,[9] has been well shown by Professor Gustav Cross,[10] who was undoubtedly right in arguing that the importance of Montaigne to Marston's play is far greater than that of those sources from which Marston drew the story and occurrences of the play. It is Montaigne who is largely responsible for shaping, and even giving expression to, Marston's dramatisation of man's attitude to certain bodily functions.

Few plays are focused more intently and more persistently on the functions of reproduction and excretion than is *The Dutch Courtesan*. Jarry's scatology might shock more sharply in the opening of *Ubu Roi*, but he does not, as does Marston, make this aspect of man's being the focal point of his play. Marston is, like the barber-surgeon he describes, a "cunning privie searcher".[11] Marston's achievement is quite remarkable if the appalling difficulty of his task is taken into account. Inevitably he has been thought to take delight in filth for its own sake and to be concerned only with titillation, but though there are words and expressions that are earthy, the play as a whole is not scatological, and it is too blunt to titillate.

Marston's debt to Montaigne is extensive and pervasive and it has been well documented. The number of parallels and allusions can be increased almost indefinitely, and they are to be traced especially to the fifth essay of the third book, "Upon some verses of *Virgil*".[12] These allusions are very frequent and very obvious, and it is plain

[9] All quotations from Florio's translation are taken from the Everyman edition of Montaigne's *Essays* (n.d., but Waller's introduction is dated 1910).

[10] K. G. W. Cross, "Marston, Montaigne, and Morality: *The Dutch Courtesan* Reconsidered", in *E.L.H.* XXVII, pp. 30–43. Cross takes up a suggestion made by Paul M. Zall in *E.L.H.*, XX, pp. 186–93.

[11] *The Dutch Courtesan*, II. III. 56. All subsequent references to the present edition are cited as *D.C.*

[12] The first and major list of parallels was reported by Charles Crawford in *Collectanea: Second Series* (1907). Others have been noted by Harvey Wood and Wine in their editions and by J. Sainmont, *Influence de Montaigne sur Marston et Webster* (1914), and A. Jose Axelrad, *Un Malcontent Elizabéthain: John Marston (1576–1634)* (1955). To these one might add Montaigne's statement: "Are there not women daily seene amongst us, who for the only profit of their husbands . . . make sale of their honesty?" (III. 94; cf. *D.C.* III. III. 8–12); and perhaps "Fidlers are often had Mongst people that are sad" (III. 67; suggested at *D.C.*, II. III. 111–15.).

that Marston soaked himself in Montaigne's work, especially in the Virgil essay. This is to be seen not only in the direct quotations but in the lines of thought in the Montaigne that are to be found reflected in the characterisation and dramatisation of *The Dutch Courtesan*. Indeed, one wonders whether the contrasts that Caputi noted may not be due as much to Montaigne's influence as to Jonson's.

The nature of Montaigne's subject—love and lust—in itself demands contrast but the whole style of Marston's play is well described in this line of Montaigne's: "Unpleasant things, and sowre matters should be sweetned and made pleasant with sportful mixtures".[13] The characters of Freevill and Malheureux are suggested by the contrast that immediately follows: "I love a lightsome and civill discretion, and loathe a roughnes and austerity of behaviour: suspecting every peevish and way ward countenance," and similarly, shortly after: "I hate a way ward and sad disposition, that glideth over the pleasures of his life, and fastens and feeds on miseries."[14] One final reference may suggest the paradox that Marston sets out to dramatise, a paradox that goes beyond the simple opposition of lust and love:

> Those who misknow themselves, may feed themselves with false approbations; but not I, who see and search my selfe into my very bowels, and know full well what belongs unto me.[15]

It is in these aspects of Montaigne's *Essays*, rather than in actual parallels and quotations, important though they are, or in the similarities of vocabulary,[16] that the nature and importance of Marston's debt to Montaigne can most clearly be seen. *The Dutch Courtesan* is indeed a searching into the very bowels.

[13] *Essays*, III. 66.
[14] *Op. cit.*, III. 67.
[15] *Op. cit.*, III. 69.
[16] There are many words in Florio's translation of Montaigne which, though by no means peculiar to that work, may well have suggested themselves to Marston. The word "firebrands", for example, appears several times and it also lies behind the name of Tysefew. The stinking breath that "Hieron's wife" supposed to be "a quality common to all men" *Essays* (III. 94) may have suggested the nostrils that smelled "worse then a putrified maribone" (*D.C.* III. I. 19) and the servant who picked his master's pocket (*Essays*, III. 76) may have put Marston in mind of this common practice. Words and expressions such as "cupping glasses", "mentula", "An armour must be hammered out", "hammered out" again, later on, and "The more steps and degrees there are" (*Essays* III. 67, 79, 90, 96 and 110) may have suggested *D.C.* IV. VI. 2 f, IV. III. 4, I. I. 7 f, and III. II. 44 f.

But, just as Marston made important changes in adapting Montreulx's story, relegating the theme of friendship to a secondary place
and making Malheureux as wretched as his name because of the situation
he has brought upon himself (rather than presenting a man made
malheureux because of misfortune[17]), so also he adapted Montaigne.

The most obvious change is that to be found in Marston's dramatisation of a marriage based on true and deeply-felt love between
Beatrice and Freevill whereas to Montaigne:

> *I see no mariages faile sooner, or more troubled, then such as are*
> *concluded for beauties sake, and hudled up for amorous desires.*[18]

There is, however, a much more subtle difference, but one which is
fundamental to what Marston dramatises and the way he sets about his
task, and which, ultimately, points to the flaw in an otherwise remarkable and successful work of art.

Although Montaigne realises that there are comic, or at least,
ridiculous aspects to man's attitude to sex (for example in the delight-
ful story he tells of what happened when his young daughter came
across an obscene word in a book she was reading aloud,[19]) it would
not be distorting what he says too much to say that he is concerned
chiefly with the relationship of love and lust. It is these two issues
that Cross argues are raised in *The Dutch Courtesan*:

> The play is clearly a morality based on a conflict between lust and
> love, between love for a courtezan and love for a friend, in terms
> of the opposition of Stoic and anti-Stoic.[20]

Marston's concerns are, however, more complex than this. In
the first place he is at pains to ensure that we are aware of the excretory
functions as well as the sexual and time after time the diseases of
venery are mentioned (especially by Cocledemoy). We cannot
avoid being aware of filth and disease at the same time as we are asked
to consider aspects of love. The reference to the wise man in his belly
act or the philosopher on the stool, and Cocledemoy's exclamations

[17] A reminiscence of the original story is to be found at *D.C.* v. ii. 89, where
Malheureux is said to be "ill fortun'd".

[18] *Essays*, iii. 73.

[19] *Op. cit.*, iii. 80.

[20] *E.L.H.*, xxvii, p. 42.

(one of which is taken from Montaigne[21]) are not prurient self-indulgence "quite out of place" in the drama.[22] They form part of a total view of man's functions which it is Marston's concern to dramatise and, in the complaint Crispinella makes about kissing, to criticise.

The closeness of the association between the different kinds of bodily function is nowhere better and more subtly seen than in Tysefew's protestation of his love for Crispinella when he says to her:

> If I have not as religiously vowd my hart to you, been drunke to your health, swalowd flap-dragons, eate glasses, drunke urine, stabd armes, and don all the offices of protested gallantrie for your sake.[23]

This "filth" is of two kinds, one natural, one the result of excess.

Then, as Paul M. Zall has remarked, Marston presents love in three ways: love is idealised as virtue; it is presented as a normal, natural "affection"; and it is shown as lust or abnormal "affection".[24]

Obviously, in *The Dutch Courtesan*, this idealised love is to be found in that of Beatrice and Freevill; the normal in that of Crispinella and Tysefew; and the abnormal in Franschina and Malheureux and also to a lesser extent, through Mary Faugh and in Cocledemoy's approaches to Franschina and Mistress Mulligrub, and in the latter's own comments on her experiences of love outside marriage.

Marston's dramatisation is much more subtle than these clear-cut distinctions suggest, of course. Freevill's attitude to love, and his varied experience of it, is very different from that of Beatrice and in him one sees much that is normal rather than ideal. Cocledemoy's bargaining with Franschina is hardly to be seen in the same light as Malheureux's, the comic undercutting the lustful.

Thus, *The Dutch Courtesan* is not simply a play with a serious main plot and a comic sub-plot for Marston employs three styles or modes in which to dramatise his attitudes to ideal and normal love and to lust. These may be called Romantic (or perhaps even Heroic), for the higher-flown flights of the Beatrice-Freevill relationship; quasi-tragic (or, more often, melodramatic) for the Franschina-Malheureux relationship; and comic. The comic is quite easily the

---

[21] *D.C.*, III. III. 44.

[22] So John Peter, *Scrutiny*, XVII, p. 152. He is one of a number of those whose complaints of coarseness in Marston are quoted and rejected by Cross (*E.L.H.* XXVII, p. 31).

[23] *D.C.*, IV. I. 58–61.   [24] *E.L.H.*, XX, p. 188.

strongest and most pervasive of these three. It undercuts the melo-drama (so that Francischina's Anglo-Dutch is a total inhibition to our ever taking her as a serious threat); it is the mode whereby the normality of the relationship between Crispinella and Tysefew is expressed; it intrudes (as Caputi noted[25]) even into Freevill's high-flown profession of love for Beatrice:

> Freevill, like all good Romeos, is carried away by verbal ex-travagance. But, significantly, he perceives his fault and breaks off in the middle of a word.

The word is "ostent"[26] and the line that follows is amusingly de-flatory: "Vaine boasts of beauties: soft joyes and the rest."

In addition, all Cocledemoy's activities are comic. Many of these are not related to the theme of love although, as has already been suggested, Cocledemoy is the principal means whereby the comic aspects of venery and defecation are expressed, and he instigates the grotesquely comic attempt to make a bargain with Mistress Mulli-grub for her "other things"[27] as her husband is on the way to the scaffold.

More important, however, and overlooked by those who complain of a lack of relationship between the main and sub-plots,[28] Cocle-demoy is a *comic* version of Freevill—of the man who has come to terms with sexual desires.

How successful is this tripartite dramatisation of Marston's view of sexuality?

Up to a point Marston succeeds brilliantly. The theme of the play is clearly expressed, the comedy is excellent—it is one of the best comic sub-plots of the period, Shakespeare's included—and Marston's concern is serious and worthwhile. Despite the occasional complaints about alleged prurience, when seen in total *The Dutch Courtesan* dramatises its difficult subject with intelligence and sensitivity. If

[25] *Caputi*, p. 235.
[26] *D.C.*, II. I. 34.
[27] *D.C.*, V. III. 91.
[28] Mulligrub and Malheureux are both hypocritical in that they affect what they do not carry out. Malheureux's "cold blood" is not unlike Mulligrub's puritanism and both are victims of Cocledemoy. Amongst many minor links, in each plot use is made of disguise and of a ring for the purpose of deception; there is praise for prostitution (by Freevill and Cocledemoy) and Mulligrub and Francischina swear revenge in an extravagant manner. See *Wine*, p. xx f.

the play fails to appeal completely it is not because we do not share sufficient common ground with Marston, nor even that modern producers and audiences are unable to respond to its serious concerns and its comic techniques, but because of flaws of two kinds, one thematic, one dramatic.

Whereas Marston's dramatisation of the normal view of sexuality is convincing and the rejection of the abnormal is well developed, Marston's presentation of ideal love is weak. In his capacity as a normal man, Freevill is as acceptable as Crispinella, but the romantic Freevill is a deception. The romantic view of Freevill as a man whose experience and maturity are such that he can indulge himself sexually without becoming a slave to passion is as unreal, and as unconvincing, as Malheureux's view of a life without passion which we see ruthlessly exposed. Furthermore there is in Beatrice a total absence of any coming to terms with that sexuality which is implicit in Marston's view of the normal state. Her response to Crispinella is typical: "Fy Crispinella you speake too broade".[29] To be convincing, Beatrice would need to be shown to be aware of the nature and demands of sensuality—a quality that we may detect in Shakespeare's Imogen and Perdita, for all their purity. As Marston has failed to invest Beatrice with such awareness, she appears to be no more than an empty romanticised ideal. It is not sufficient for Marston to parody the romantic extravagance of Freevill's praise of Beatrice, he must, to succeed completely, convince us, as does Shakespeare—and as only art can—of the practicality of an ideal.

It is, however, the dramatic weakness that is more damaging in the theatre. The tremendous vitality of the sub-plot, and the qualities of the exchanges in which Crispinella is involved, justify Wine's description of the play as a *comic* treatment of Montaigne's theme.[30] Cross percipiently states that "Marston did well to cast his study of human sexuality in the form of a tragicomedy".[31] The difficulty is that although the theme and its conception are tragicomic, its working out is almost entirely comic, and when not comic it is romantic and, to a small extent, melodramatic. The dramatic mode is not, at all points, an expression of the theme.

It has often been pointed out that Francischina[32] does not seriously

[29] *D.C.* III. I. 24.   [30] *Wine*, p. xvi.

[31] *E.L.H.*, xxvii, p. 35.

[32] Wine rightly describes her as "ridiculously vicious" (p. xix).

threaten Freevill's future and we never feel that Malheureux is in great jeopardy. Marston does well to avoid deceiving his audience and it is dramatically right that we should feel that Freevill is endeavouring to maintain control of the situation, like the Duke in *Measure for Measure*. What is wrong, however, is that we never doubt that Francischina will be foiled and Malheureux saved. It is even possible to pinpoint the most serious moment of weakness: the moment that robs the play of the essential quality that would not only enable dramatic tension to be developed logically but would serve to dramatise much more effectively the conflict between love and lust, normality and excess.

When Malheureux considers Francischina's demand that he kill Freevill,[33] he entertains this thought for less than a dozen lines before he begins to doubt and in less than twenty he has realised "how easie ti's to erre" and decided to tell Freevill all. This does Malheureux's sentiments much credit, and shows, perhaps, the strength of the influence of the concept of friendship, but the play as drama and as an expression of Marston's concerns, is seriously though by no means fatally weakened.[34] The main plot has lost its bite. We never feel, as we do in *Measure for Measure*, that the threats are serious and the implications real.

One or two minor matters deserve attention. Marston does not limit himself to matters concerning sexuality for there are brief discussions on censorship[35] and suicide.[36] In the sub-plot[37] there is a convincing naturalness about situation and dialogue that not even the extravagant comedy can obscure.[38]

On the other hand, whilst Marston is willing to condemn Francischina, he seems in no way condemnatory of Freevill's earlier behaviour. At times his expression is less than clear,[39] sometimes awkward[40] and inexact[41] and occasionally undramatic.[42]

---

[33] *D.C.* II. II. 201 f.

[34] Wine overstates his case, surely, when he says, "The picture of a man's realising that his code of life is failing him and that he is actually 'passion's slave' is one of Marston's finest achievements" (p. xvii).

[35] *D.C.*, III. I. 25 f.

[36] *D.C.*, v. II. 1 f.   [37] e.g., *D.C.*, II. III.

[38] It does not, as Wine suggests (p. xx), require the presence of Crispinella and Tysefew to make "the rest of the play believable".

[39] e.g., *D.C.*, III. I. 128–30.   [40] e.g., *D.C.*, III. I. 198–200 and v. III. 43.

[41] e.g., *D.C.*, v. III. 38.   [42] e.g., *D.C.*, v. II. 17–18.

Finally, what of Marston's attitude to his play? It is suggested in the commentary that the opening quotations from Martial might as much be directed by Marston at himself as at Malheureux. This, and the references in the Prologue to the "Slight hastie labours in this easie Play" and his rejection of the idea of instructing as well as delighting, must be taken with a pinch of salt. Marston in *The Dutch Courtesan* is seriously and didactically concerned with human fundamentals, and if the play is not quite the masterpiece it might have been, it is, nevertheless, especially in its comedy, a very fine dramatisation of the paradox of sensuality.

A NOTE ON THE TEXT

There were two editions of *The Dutch Courtesan* in Marston's lifetime, in 1605 and 1633, but only the first has any authority, and this serves as the copy-text for this edition. It was entered in the Stationers' Register on 26 June 1605, printed by T[homas] P[urfoot],[1] and sold by John Hodgets. Twelve copies are extant: British Museum (2), Bodleian, Victoria and Albert Museum (Dyce copy and one other), Pforzheimer, Boston Public Library, Harvard, Chapin, Folger, Huntington, and Library of Congress. All have been collated as the basis for this edition.

The collation and description are: 4°: A-H⁴; A1r title page; A1v blank; A2r *Prologue* and Fabulæ argumentum; A2v *Dramatis personæ* (the characters *not* being so arranged that the female characters follow the male); A3r-H4r Text; H4v blank.

The only other edition prepared according to contemporary editorial practices is that of Martin L. Wine.[2] A number of readings from the editions of Halliwell-Phillipps, Bullen, Walley and Wilson, and H. Harvey Wood have been incorporated in this edition. I am also indebted to J. Le Gay Brereton, for certain conjectural readings.

Dr Wine (following Greg) notes that the 1605 quarto "seems to have been printed in two parts: A-E, F-H" but, on the grounds of similarity of type, he argues for a single printing house. He suggests two compositors and possibly two presses for A-E, and then, for F-H, the "removal of one compositor" and the use of one press suggesting, he believes, a need for less haste in preparing these last three sheets. This removal of one compositor may also explain the one-press operation on sheet D. Dr Wine finds nothing conclusive from spelling analysis but argues that the use of colons to conclude some speech headings points to two different compositorial habits. The source of the quarto, is, he believes, "almost certainly the author's

[1] W. W. Greg, *A Bibliography of the English Printed Drama to the Restoration*, vol. I. p. 338 f. Also vol. III. pp. 1089-91.
[2] Regents Renaissance Drama Series (1965).

fair copy or a copy very closely related to it" and he considers the state of the stage directions "indicates the author's real concern over production." Exits and Entrances he considers to be, in general, well marked and the substantive correction "is not heavy". He suggests B inner and G inner may have been corrrected by Marston "but reference to the manuscript copy is also very possible". He states that his edition records "the variants among the corrected and uncorrected formes in the various copies".

I would modify these conclusions.

The play was certainly set in two parts, A-E and F-H, but there is nothing to indicate a division in running off. The watermarks of the Dyce and the two B.M. copies are of two kinds, a clover and a hand with star, and these, where watermarks appear, occur in each of these copies and in both sections of the setting. The same kind of type seems to have been used for setting each part but I am by no means convinced that the same cases of type were used for F-H as for the earlier sheets (though very variable inking makes type identification difficult). This is in accord with the suggestion I shall make that the compositor who set F-H was not involved in A-E.

Two skeleton formes were constructed for A-E but their use was irregular. The order through the press was probably Ai, Ao; then, pretty certainly, Bi, Bo, Ci, Co, Do, Di, Eo, Ei. As would be expected the major variants appear in Bi, Ci, and Eo but for D the major variants appear in Di which went second to the press of this pair. D, however, is unusual. It went through two stages of correction[3] and the same set of running titles was used for each of its formes. This same set was also used for Ci and Ei and it was derived from three running titles used for Bo and a running title that had been used in Ai and Ao. Indeed this particular title appears in Ai, Ao, Bo, Ci, Do, Di, and Ei.

As Dr Wine says, spelling tests are inconclusive but there are one or two unusual spellings that just may—added to what has so far been noted—suggest how A-E was set. The spelling *Sammon* appears three times on E4v (E outer) whereas *Salmon* occurs in E inner (once on E3v and twice on E4r). (It is also spelt *Salmon* twice on F1r at the very end of Act IV in a passage that could conceivably have been set (completing that Act) before the break separating A-E and F-H.)

The spelling *hyp* appears on E1v (the same forme as *Salmon*) where-

---

[3] Apparent at *D.C.*, II. III. 36.

as *hippe* appears on E1r (the same forme as *Sammon*). *Friend* (or related words) is always spelt with "ie" except on five occasions—two on B4v and three times in C1r. The only other difference of any significance in this context is not clear cut. The spelling *hart* is used throughout except on three occasions—*heart* appears on C2v (C outer), E4v (E outer) and E2r.

The spelling evidence is very slim and alone would amount to nothing. These changes may reflect the author not the compositor. Nevertheless, with the running title evidence, the spellings *frend*, *sammon*, *hippe*, and possibly *heart*, might suggest that the formes in which these entirely or chiefly occur—Co and Eo—were set by a compositor helping out the man setting the other four formes of this group. The assisting compositor might also have set B4v.

This is not a strong case, but rather than supposing two compositors and two presses for A-E, I would suggest, on the basis of the indistinct evidence that can be recovered, one compositor helped out either in pages or occasionally in whole formes, by another. In the circumstances, one press seems likely.

Dr Wine considers that the use of colons indicates compositorial idiosyncrasy although he does not use them to show how the work of the two compositors is to be apportioned. The runs of colons or stops never occur in whole signatures (as he states) and the two short runs he specifies (C1v-C3r and B3v-B4v) are broken in half a dozen places. Even if these runs were complete it would be impossible to fit them into a compositorial pattern. This usage of colons and stops (and commas) is caused by type shortage—a characteristic feature of the play.

While the spelling differences noted in A-E are slight, they are a little stronger between A-E and F-H and may be sufficient to tempt us to a conclusion. The last three sheets were all printed from one forme. Apart from variations of spelling that may be due to justification, the twenty-three pages of F-H always use the forms *Ile*, *me*, *she*, and *months*; *bee* does appear twice, *do* is much more common than *doe*, and the preference for *-esse* rather than *-es* is great.

The thirty-six pages of text in A-E show a frequent use of other forms than *Ile*; *mee*, *shee*, *monneth* and *monnethes* occur; *bee* appears fairly often, *doe* is much more frequent than *do*, and the preference of *-esse* to *-es* is slight. Gemination is more common than in F-H.

Further, the line widths and running titles in F-H are more regular than those of A-E and the Act headings (IV and V) are of the same setting of type, whereas the three act headings appearing in A-E are in a different style and setting of type, from each other and those of IV and V. In addition the frequency of turned letters in F-H is very, very, much less than in A-E, the fourth recto is regularly not signed (nor is A4) and sententiae are indicated in a different style from those in A-E. Thus, I would hazard a guess that whoever set F-H was not involved in setting A-E.

I disagree that less haste was required in setting F-H. The compositor may have been more competent (and so, as I read the evidence, did not need the help that was required by whoever set A-E) but he was certainly hard pressed by the time it came to H. This gathering is set in seven pages; eight are needed—and the eighth is blank!

H3 is not signed, and catchwords are omitted from H2v on. The number of lines per page (a maximum of 38 elsewhere) is, in H, 38, 39, 39, 39, 39, 39, 40. On the last page, *Exeunt* and *FINIS* appear crammed in the same line as the last line of text. Two speeches (one on H2v and one on H4r) have been run on to their predecessors (doubtless to save space) and there is great use of abbreviation (though this may not all be compositorial). Cocledemoy's epilogue is not separated off from the dialogue as would be expected. From the evidence of cramming it is plain that eight or nine lines of the setting should have turned over to H4v—and its use would scarcely have added to the compositor's work, for the same amount of setting would be needed and the tension involved in cramming avoided.

I can but imagine that by cramming the last pages into seven sides, the outer—H1r, H2v, H3r, and a blank H4v—could be sent to the press earlier than if it had been necessary for H4v to be set (if setting was by formes) or H3v and H4r (if setting was seriatim). As to set the few lines needed for H4v would not have taken so very long, I imagine that the setting was seriatim until, say, H2r, when, the pressmen breathing down the compositor's neck, a change was made in order to complete the outer quickly in this manner. The chronic shortage of type—especially Roman lower case "y" (for which "ie" and italic "y" are substituted)—suggests that insufficient distribution had also been done—again, a sign of haste. Also this forme may not have been proofed.

The Exits and Entrances are more deficient than Dr Wine allows; there is confusion over who gives Caqueteur the ring and over the name of Burnish-Garnish. Although some of the abbreviated words may be for compositorial convenience (in H especially), such shortening also occurs in part of the text where there is no pressure on space. Some, especially the abbreviations for Crispinella, strike me as authorial draft rather than fair copy. (Incidentally all the abbreviations except *xxtie* for twenty occur in F-H.) The positioning of words like *Farewell* (v. I. 64), Freevill's speech heading after v. II. 30, and the direction to Beatrice to faint; the very awkward lineation of songs in II. ii. and IV. vii, and the incomplete verse at III. i. 6, are some aspects of the text which do not incline me to accept Dr Wine's view that this is printed from fair copy. The cramming of directions for action into the margin of the printed version may also reflect the state of the printer's copy.

Nevertheless, Marston may well have taken some care in preparing this MS for the printer. Many sententiae are marked—though possibly Marston always did this as a matter of course—and there is that curious tag at the opening of the play. It cannot have been spoken and it is set as if reflecting a written afterthought. As my Introduction suggests, Marston may have thought it as applicable to himself as to his play.

Thus I imagine the 1605 text to have been set from a final draft of the play, not prepared fully for the theatre, but lightly prepared by Marston for the printer. In addition to what has been said about its printing, it seems likely that conscientious but inefficient proof-reading was arranged. There are about twice as many proof corrections as those listed by Dr Wine (he notes forty-five against this edition's ninety-six) but even then, the proof-reader missed, or the compositor failed to correct, an inordinate number of typographical errors, not to speak of literary errors. Every forme exists in a variant state (though the variants in Ai and Ho may be fortuitous—in the circumstances of haste described regarding Ho, it may not have been proofed and v. III. 53 may be due to poor make-ready) but three times as many letters are left upside down as are corrected. Nevertheless, someone seems to have checked the copy in order to make certain corrections (such as that at IV. III. 17) even if, as Cocledemoy's ghost entry after I. II. 57 shows, they are occasionally erroneous.

In view of this I have felt encouraged to make one or two substantive changes and to re-allocate some speeches, that, if the copy had been fair and the printing conditions regular, I should have been tempted to leave unaltered, especially in an edition of this kind which is intended to stick closely to the original in spelling and lineation. Where the copy seems to have been consulted in proof-reading I have been a little more willing to accept corrections than has Dr Wine. The more important changes can be justified in the following manner.

Although the language at II. II. 94 is English[4], this line has been given to Franceschina. Her Anglo-Dutch is highly inconsistent—she uses *my* instead of *min* twice at II. II. 195, and *with* appears at II. II. 73. If this line is Freevill's, "With all my hart Sir" is awkward, even allowing for the conventionality of the expression. The passage beginning IV. VII. 91 has also been re-allocated (and the usual re-allocations of I. I. 50, 54; IV. I. 4; IV. VII. 13; and V. II. 57 have been made).

The most interesting substantival emendations are two related to the sound of the numeral *one*. At II. I. 87, *once* has been emended to *one's* (= one is); at III. II. 25, I have taken up Bullen's suggestion (Wun') and emended *One a* to *Wan' a*.[5]

I have, unlike Dr Wine, assumed that the corrections at I. II. 23 and II. I. 157 are sound as the copy may have been checked with the setting about this point (Dr Wine suggesting that Marston possibly checked this forme). Dr Wine perciently suggests that music was played between certain acts (see his note to II. III. 111) and this seems to me to require *Worship* at IV. VII. 117 to be in the plural. My reading of III. IV. 63-4 is very different from Dr Wine's (whose recording of the variants at this point is incorrect):

Q 1605: I must haue the Sammon to, worship: *Cocledemoy*, now . . .

Wine: I must have the salmon to worship. Cocledemoy, now . . .

This ed.: I must have the Sammon to. Worshipfull *Cocledemoy*, now . . .

Here *to* = also. *Worshipfull* is frequently abbreviated to *Worsh.* (and at V. III. 134 even with a lower case *w*).

The commentary on I. II. 63-4, II. I. 9, III. IV. 54, IV. III. 26, might also be consulted in this context.

This edition is based on the Quarto of 1605. I have accepted the corrections made in that edition except for Cocledemoy's unnecessary

---

[4] As at *D.C.*, II. II. 100 f. 121, 129 f, etc.
[5] Cf., use of this sound at *D.C.* III. I. 104—*on's*; and, in Anglo-Dutch, *on* at IV. IV. 40. Similarly 'wan' stands for 'won' in *I Henry IV* Q1 (III. II. 59).

entry at I. II. 57. Most of the emendations are of punctuation and accidentals; speech prefixes and stage directions have been altered or added in order to make the text actable. The substantival changes are relatively few and the more interesting ones have been discussed above. In making them I have been guided by my conjectural reconstruction of the process of transmission of the text.

Textual Notes appear in two places. Those changes affecting accidentals and substantives which alter meaning are recorded at the foot of the page on which they appear. All remaining variants and emendations are listed in the Textual Notes on pp. 89-94. Turned letters (other than "u" and "n") have not been recorded unless the subject of correction in 1605; neither has the distinction between long and short "s": otherwise the lemma has been given in the same form as in the source from which it was taken.

Stage directions which have been added have been placed within pointed brackets. Roman square brackets have been used to isolate stage directions occurring in the middle of a line of text.

The following silent alterations have been made and are not recorded in the Notes:

(a) the letter "s" has been substituted for "long s" wherever it occurs;

(b) the complementary letters "i" and "j", "u" and "v", "vv" and "w" have been interchanged in conformity with modern practice;

(c) all regular abbreviations have been expanded;

(d) speech-prefixes are set in caps, and are given in full and always in the same form;

(e) names of characters are similarly normalised in the text and in stage directions;

(f) except for turned "n" and "u" (which cannot readily be distinguished in this text) typographic errors, such as wrong fount, turned (unless the subject of correction in 1605), reversed, or broken letters have been corrected;

(g) spacing variations, unless the subject of correction in 1605, have been superseded.

(h) turned apostrophes in F-G-H have been corrected (although sententiae have been indicated in the two styles of the quarto);

(i) initial capitalisation of lines of verse and after terminal punctuation has been introduced (e.g. after ? and !);

(*j*) final stops have been introduced at end of speeches;

(*k*) relineation of prose (though the layout of the prose has been retained wherever possible). Where relineation involves re-duction of initial capital letters, this is noted;

(*l*) the form of noting the beginnings and ends of acts.

All other departures from the Copy-Text are recorded in the Textual Notes.

PROLOGUE

Slight hastie labours in this easie Play,
Present not what you would, but what we may:
For this vouchsafe to know the onely end
Of our now studie is, not to offend.
Yet thinke not, but like others raile we could,   5
(Best art Presents, not what it can, but should)
And if our pen in this seeme over slight,
We strive not to instruct, but to delight,
As for some few, we know of purpose here
To taxe, and scowt: know firme art cannot feare   10
Vaine rage: onely the highest grace we pray
Is, you'le not taxe, untill you judge our Play.
Thinke and then speake: tis rashnesse, and not wit
To speake what is in passion, and not judgement fit:
Sit then, with faire exspectance, and survay   15
Nothing but passionate man in his slight play,
Who hath this onely ill: to some deem'd worst,
A modest diffidence, and selfe mistrust.

FABULAE ARGUMENTUM

*The difference betwixt the love of a Curteȝan, and a wife, is the full
scope of the Play, which intermixed with the deceits of a wittie Citie
Jester, fils up the Comedie.*

DRAMATIS PERSONAE

FRANCISCHINA, *A Dutch Curteʒan.*

MARY FAUGH, *An old woman.*

SIR LIONELL FREEVILL ⎫
⎬ *Two old Knights.*
SIR HUBERT SUBBOYS ⎭

YOUNG FREEVILL, SIR LIONELLS *Sonne.*

BEATRICE ⎫
⎬ SIR HUBERTS *Daughters.*
CRISPINELLA ⎭

PUTIFER, *Their Nurse.*

TYSEFEW, *A blunt Gallant.*

CAQUETEUR, *A pratling Gull.*

MALHEUREUX, YOUNG FREEVILLS *unhappie friend.*

COCLEDEMOY, *A knavishly witty City companion.*

MAISTER MULLIGRUB, *A Vintner.*

MISTRESSE MULLIGRUB, *His wife.*

MAISTER BURNISH, *A Goldsmith.*

LIONELL, *His man.*

HOLIFERNES RAINS-CURE, *A Barbers boy.*

Three WATCHMEN, ⟨*three* PAGES, GENTLEMEN *with music,* HALBERDIERS, CHRISTIAN, *a* SERVANT *and* OFFICERS⟩.

*Turpe est
difficiles
habere
nugas.*

Enter 3. PAGES *with lightes.* MULLIGRUB, FREEVILL,
MALHEUREUX, TYSEFEW, *and* CAQUETEUR.

FREEVILL. Nay comfort my good hoast *Sharke,* my good
Mulligrub.

MALHEUREUX. Advance thy snout, doe not suffer thy sorrowful
nose to droppe on thy spanish leather jerkin, most hardly honest
Mulligrub.   5

FREEVILL. What, cogging *Cocledemoy* is runne away with a
neast of goblets, true, what then? They will be hammerd out well
enough, I warrant you.

MULLIGRUB. Sure, some wise man would finde them out
presently.   10

FREEVILL. Yes sure, if we could finde out some wiseman
presently.

MALHEUREUX. How was the plate lost? How did it vanish?

FREEVILL. In most sincere prose thus: that man of much money,
some witte, but lesse honestie, cogging *Cocledemoy,* comes this   15
night late into mine hostes *Mulligrubs* Taverne heere, cals for
a roome, the house being ful, *Cocledemoy* consorted with his
moveable chattle, his instrument of fornication, the bawde Mrs
Mary Faugh, are imparlarde next the streete, good poultrie was
their foode, blackbird, Larke, woodcocke, and mine hoast here,   20
comes in, cryes God blesse you, and departes: A blinde Harper
enters, craves audience, uncaseth, playes, the Drawer for female
privatnes sake is nodded out, who knowing that whosoever will
hit the mark of profit, must like those that shoot in stone-bowes
winke with one eye, growes blind a the right side and departs.   25

CAQUETEUR. He shal answere for that winking with one eye at
the last day.

MALHEUREUX. Let him have day till then, and he will winke
with both his eyes.

FREEVILL. *Cocledemoy* perceiving none in the roome but the 30
blind Harper (whose eyes heaven had shut up, from beholding
wickednesse,) unclaspes a casement to the street very patiently,
pockets up 3. bowles unnaturally, thrustes his wench forth the
window, and him selfe most preposterously with his heeles
forward followes: the unseeing Harper playes on, bids the empty 35
dishes and the treacherous candles much good do them. The
Drawer returns, but out alas, not onely the birdes, but also the
neast of goblets were flowne away, Laments are raisde.

TYSEFEW. Which did not pierce the heavens.

FREEVILL. The Drawers mone, mine hoast doth crie, the bowles 40
are gone.

MULLIGRUB. *Hic finis Priami.*

MALHEUREUX. Nay, be not jaw-falne, my most sharking *Mulli-*
grub.

FREEVILL. Tis your just affliction, remember the sinnes of the 45
sellar, and repent, repent.

MULLIGRUB. I am not jawfalne, but I will hang the conicatching
Cocledemoy, and theres an end of't.

Exit.

CAQUETEUR. Is it a right stone, it shewes well by candlelight.

⟨TYSEFEW.⟩ So doe many thinges that are counterfeite, but I 50
assure you this is a right Diamond.

CAQUETEUR. Might I borrow it of you, it will not a little grace
my finger in visitation of my Mistresse.

⟨TYSEFEW.⟩ Why use it most sweet *Caqueteur*, use it.

CAQUETEUR. Thankes good Sir. Ti's growne high night: 55
Gentles, rest to you.

Exit.

TYSEFEW. A torch! Sound wench, soft sleepe, and sanguine
dreames to you both. On boy!

⟨*Exit.*⟩

FREEVILL. Let me bid you good rest.

MALHEUREUX. Not so trust me, I must bring my friend home: I 60
dare not give you up to your owne companie, I feare the warmth
of wine and youth, will draw you to some Common house of
lascivious entertainement.

FREEVILL. Most necessarie buildings *Malheureux*. Ever since my
    intention of Marriage, I doe pray for their continuance.   65
MALHEUREUX. Lov'd Sir, your reason?
FREEVILL. Marry least my house should be made one: I would
    have married men love the Stewes, as Englishmen lov'd the low
    Countreys: wish war should be maintain'd there, least it should
    come home to their owne dores: what, suffer a man to have a hole   70
    to put his head in, though hee goe to the Pillorie for it: Youth
    and Appetite are above the Clubbe of *Hercules*.
MALHEUREUX. This lust is a most deadly sinne sure.
FREEVILL. Nay, tis a most lively sinne sure.
MALHEUREUX. Well I am sure, tis one of the head sinnes.   75
FREEVILL. Nay, I am sure it is one of the middle sinnes.
MALHEUREUX. Pitie, tis growne a most dayly vice.
FREEVILL. But a more nightly vice, I assure you.
MALHEUREUX. Well, tis a sinne.
FREEVILL. I, or else few men would wish to go to Heaven: and   80
    not to disguise with my friend, I am now going the way of all
    flesh.
MALHEUREUX. Not to a Curtezan?
FREEVILL. A courteous one.
MALHEUREUX. What to a Sinner?   85
FREEVILL. A verie Publican.
MALHEUREUX. Deere my lov'd friend, let mee bee full with you.
    Know Sir, the strongest argument that speakes
    Against the soules eternitie is lust,
    That Wisemans folly, and the fooles wisedome: 90
    But to grow wild in loose lasciviousnesse,
    Given up to heat, and sensuall Appetite:
    Nay to expose your health, and strength, and name,
    Your precious time, and with that time the hope
    Of due preferment advantageous meanes,   95
    Of any worthy end to the stale use,
    The common bosome of a money Creature,
    One that sels humane flesh: a Mangonist.
FREEVILL. Alas good creatures, what would you have them doe?
    Would you have them get their living by the curse of man, the   100
    sweat of their browes? So they doe, everie man must follow his

    64 *Malheureux*. Ever] Malheureus euer Q.

trade, and everie woman her occupation. A poore decayed
mechanicall mans wife, her husband is layd up, may not she law-
fully be layd downe, when her husbands onely rising, is by his
wifes falling? A Captaines wife wants meanes, her Commander 105
lyes in open field abroad, may not she lye in civile armes at home?
A waighting Gentlewoman that had wont to take say to her Lady,
miscaries, or so: the Court misfortune throwes her downe, may
not the Citie curtesie take her up? Doe you know no Alderman
would pitie such a womans case? Why is charity growne a sinne? 110
Or releeving the poore and impotent an offence? You will say
beasts take no money for their fleshly entertainment: true, because
they are beasts, therefore beastly, onely men give to loose,
because they are men, therefore manly: and indeede, wherein
should they bestow their money better? In Land, the title may be 115
crackt: In Houses, they may bee burnt: In apparell, twill weare:
In wine, alas for pitie our throate is but short: But employ your
money upon women, and a thousand to nothing, some one of
them will bestow that on you, which shall sticke by you as long
as you live; they are no ingratefull persons, they will give quite 120
for quo: do ye protest, they'le sweare, doe you rise, theyle fall,
doe you fall, they'le rise, do you give them, the french Crowne,
they'le give you the french; *O iustus iusta iustum.* They sell their
bodies: doe not better persons sell their soules? Nay, since all
things have been sould, honor, justice, faith: nay, even God 125
himselfe: Aye me, what base ignoblenesse is it, to sell the
pleasure of a wanton bed.
Why doe men scrape, why heape to full heapes joyne,
But for his Mistresse, who would care for coyne,
For this I hold to be deny'd of no man,   130
All thinges are made for man, and man for woman; give me my
                                                              fee.

MALHEUREUX.   Of ill you merite well: my hearts good friend,
Leave yet at length, at length, for know this ever
Tis no such sinne to erre, but to persever.

FREEVILL.   Beautie is womans vertue, love the lifes Musique: and 135
woman the daintines or second course of heavens curious work-
manship, since then beauty, love and women are good, how can
the love of womans beawty be bad? And, *Bonum quo communius
eo melius,* wil't then goe with me?

MALHEUREUX. Whether?

FREEVILL. To a house of salvation.

MALHEUREUX. Salvation?

FREEVILL. Yes 'twill make thee repent. Wil't goe to the family of
love? I will shew thee my creature: a pretty nimble eyd Dutch
Tanakin; An honest soft-hearted impropriation, a soft plumpe, 145
round cheekt froe, that has beauty inough, for her vertue, vertue
enough for a woman, and woman enough for any reasonable man
in my knowledg: wil't passe a long with me?

MALHEUREUX. What to a Brothell, to behold an impudent
prostitution? Fye on't I shall hate the whole sex to see her: the 150
most odious spectacle the earth can present, is an immodest
vulger woman.

FREEVILL. Good still: my braine shall keep't: you must goe as
you love me.

MALHEUREUX. Well: Ile go to make her loath the shame shee's
in. 155
The sight of vice augments the hate of sinne.

FREEVILL. The sight of vice augments the hate of sinne, very
fine perdy.

Exeunt.

SCENE II

Enter COCLEDEMOY, *and* MARY FAUGH.

COCLEDEMOY. *Mary, Mary Faugh.*

MARY FAUGH. Hem.

COCLEDEMOY. Come my worshipfull Rotten Rough bellide
Baud, ha my blew tooth'd Patrones of naturall wickednesse, give
me the gobletts. 5

MARY FAUGH. By yea, and by nay, maister *Cocledemoy* I feare
you'le play the knave and restore them.

COCLEDEMOY. No by the Lord *Aunt*, Restitution is Catholique
and thou know'st we love.

MARY FAUGH. What? 10

COCLEDEMOY. Oracles are seas'd: *Tempus preteritum,* do'st
heare my worshipfull glisterpipe, thou ungodly fyer that burnt
Dianas Temple, do'st heare Baud?

B

MARY FAUGH. In very good truthnes you are the foulest
mouth'd prophaine railing Brother, call a woman the most 15
ungodly names: I must confesse we all eate of the forbidden fruite,
and for mine owne part tho I am one of the family of love and as
they say a bawd that covers the multitude of sinnes, yet I trust I
am none of the wicked that eate fish a Fridaies.

COCLEDEMOY. Hang toastes, I raile at thee my worshipfull 20
organ bellowes that fills the pipes, my fine ratling fleamy cough a
the lunges and cold with a Pox, I raile at thee: what my right
pretious pandres supportres of *Barbar Surgeons* and inhauntres
of *lotium* and dyet drinke: I raile at thee necessary damnation, Ile
make an oration, I, in praise of thy most courtly in fashion, and 25
most pleasureable function, I.

MARY FAUGH. I prethee do, I love to heare my selfe prais'd, as
well as any old Ladie, I.

COCLEDEMOY. *List then*, a Baud, first for her profession or
vocation it is most worshipfull of all the 12. Companies, for as 30
that trade is most honorable that sells the best commodityes, as
the Draper is more worshipfull then the poyntmaker, the silke-
man more worshipfull then the Draper, and the Goldsmith more
honorable then both, *Little Mary*: so the Baud above all, her shop
has the best ware, for where these sell but cloath, sattens, and 35
jewels, shee sels divine vertues as virginitie, modestie and such
rare Jemmes, and those not like a petty chapman, by retaile, but
like a great marchant by whole sale, *wa, ha, ho*, and who are her
customers, not base corn cutters, or sowgelders, but most rare
wealthie Knightes, and most rare bountifull Lordes are her custo- 40
mers. Againe, where as no trade or vocation profiteth, but by the
losse and displeasure of another, as the Marchant thrives not but
by the licentiousnes of giddie, and unsetled youth: the Lawyer,
but by the vexation of his client, the Phisition, but by the maladies
of his patient, onely my smoothe gumbde Bawd lives by others 45
pleasure, and onely growes rich by others rising. O merciful
gaine, O righteous in-come. So much for her vocation, trade

I. II. 23 inhauntres] Q^e; inhauncres Q^u.   25 thy] Q^e; the Q^u.
26 function] Q^e; functis Q^u.   27 heare] Q^e; haue Q^u.
28 Ladie] Q^e; Iade Q^u.

43 giddie, and unsetled youth:] giddie youth, and vnsetled: Q^u; giddie, and
vn̥setled youth: Q^e.

and life, as for their death, how can it bee bad, since their
wickednesse is always before their eyes, and a deathes head
most commonly on their middle finger. To conclude, ti's most 50
certaine they must needes both live well, and dye well, since most
commonly they live in *Clearken-well*, and dye in *Bridewell*.
Dixi Mary.

Enter FREEVILL *and* MALHEUREUX.

FREEVILL. Come along, yonders the preface or exordium to my
wench, the bawde: Fetch, fetch. ⟨*Exit* MARY.⟩ What M. 55
Cocledemoy, is your knaveshippe yet stirring, looke to it,
Mulligrub lyes for you.
COCLEDEMOY. The more foole he, I can lye for my selfe,
worshipfull friend, hang toastes, I vannish. Ha my fine boy thou
art a scholler, and hast read *Tullies Offices*, my fine knave, hang 60
toastes.
FREEVILL. The Vintner will toast you and he catch you.
COCLEDEMOY. I will draw the Vintner to the stoope, and when
he runs low tilt him. Ha my fine knave, art going to thy
recreation? 65
FREEVILL. Yes my capriceous raskall.
COCLEDEMOY. Thou wilt looke like a foole then by and by.
FREEVILL. Looke like a foole why?
COCLEDEMOY. Why according to the old saying, A begger when
he is lowsing of himselfe lookes like a Philosopher, a hard bound 70
Philosopher, when he is on the stoole, lookes like a tyrant, and a
wise man, when hee is in his belly act, lookes like a foole. God
give your worship good rest, grace and mercy keepe your *Syring*
straight, and your *Lotium* unspilt.

⟨*Exit*.⟩

Enter FRANCISCHINA.

FREEVILL. See, Sir this is she. 75
MALHEUREUX. This?
FREEVILL. This.
MALHEUREUX. A Curtesan? Now cold bloud defend me, what a
proportion afflictes me?

57f. no S.D.] Qᵘ; *Enter Cocledemoy*. Qᶜ. 63 stoope] Qᶜ; sloope Qᵘ.
76 This?] Qᶜ; ∼. Qᵘ. 77 This.] Qᶜ; ∼? Qᵘ.

FRANCISCHINA.   O mine aderliver love, vat sall me do to requit   80
dis your mush affection.

FREEVILL.   Marry salute my friend, clippe his necke, and kisse
him welcome.

FRANCISCHINA.   A mine art, Sir you bin very velcome.

FREEVILL.   Kisse her man with a more familiar affection, so.   85
Come what entertainement? Goe to your Lute.

Exit FRANCISCHINA.

And how dost approve my somtimes elected? Shees none of
your ramping Cannibals, that devoure mans flesh, nor any of
your curtian gulfes, that will never be satisfied, untill the best
thing a man has be throwne into them. I lov'd her with my heart   90
untill my soule shewed me the imperfection of my body, and
placed my affection on a lawful love, my modest *Beatrice*, which
if this short heeles knew, there were no being for mee with eyes
before her face. But faith, dost thou not somewhat excuse my
sometimes incontinency with her enforcive beauties? Speake.   95

MALHEUREUX.   Hah, she is a whore, is she not?

FREEVILL.   Whore? Fie whore? You may call her a Curtezan, a
Cocatrice, or (as that worthy spirite of an eternall happinesse
saide) a Suppositarie, but whore? Fie: tis not in fashion to call
things by their right names. Is a great marchant, a coockold?   100
You must say, he is one of the livery. Is a great Lord, a foole?
You must say, he is weake. Is a gallant pocky? You must say, he
has the court skab. Come shees your mistresse or so.

Enter FRANCISCHINA *with her Lute.*

Come Syren your voice.

FRANCISCHINA.   Vill not you stay in mine bosome to night love?   105

FREEVILL.   By no meanes sweet breast, this Gentleman has
vowde to see me chastly layde.

FRANCISCHINA.   He shall have a bedde too, if dat it please him.

FREEVILL.   Peace you tender him offence, hee is one of a professed abstinence, Syren your voyce and away.   110

She singes to her Lute.

THE SONG.

The darke is my delight,
  So tis the Nightingales.
My Musicke's in the night,
  So is the Nightingales.
My body is but little,   115
  So is the Nightingales.
I love to sleepe gainst prickle,
  So doth the Nightingale.

⟨FREEVILL.⟩   Thankes, Busse, so the night growes old. Good
  rest.   120
FRANCISCHINA.   Rest to mine deare love, rest, and no long
  absence.
FREEVILL.   Beleeve me not long.
FRANCISCHINA.   Sall Ick not beleeve you long.

                              Exit FRANCISCHINA.

FREEVILL.   O yes, come viah, away, boy, on.   125

                              Exit his PAGE *lighting him.*

⟨Re-⟩enter FREEVILL *and seemes to overheare* MALHEUREUX.

MALHEUREUX.   Is she unchast, can such a one be damde?
  O love and beautie, yee two eldest seedes
  Of the vast Chaos, what strong right you have,
  Even in thinges divine, our very soules.
FREEVILL ⟨*aside*⟩.   *Wha, ha, ho,* come bird come, stand peace.   130
MALHEUREUX.   Are strumpets then such things, so delicate,
  Can custome spoile, what nature made so good?
  Or is their Custome bad? Beauti's for use,
  I never saw a sweet face vitious,
  It might be proud, inconstant, wanton, nice,   153
  But never tainted with unnaturall vice.
  Their worst is, their best art is love to winne,
  „O that to love should be or shame, or sinne.
FREEVILL ⟨*aside*⟩.   By the Lord hee's caught. Laughter eternall?
MALHEUREUX.   Soule I must love her: desteny is weake to my
                              affection.   140

A common love, blush not faint breast
That which is ever loved of most is best.
Let colder eld the strongst objections move,
No lov's without some lust, no life without some love.

FREEVILL.   Nay come on good sir, what though the most odious 145
spectacle the world can present be an immodest vulgar woman:
Yet sir for my sake.

MALHEUREUX.   Well sir for your sake Ile thinke better of them.

FREEVILL.   Doe good sir and pardon me that have brought you
in
You knowe the sight of vice augments the hate of sinne.   150

MALHEUREUX.   Hah? Will you go home sir 'tis hye bed time?

FREEVILL.   With all my hart sir only do not chide me.
I must confesse.

MALHEUREUX.   A wanton lover you have been.

FREEVILL.   O that to love should be or shame, or sinne.   155

MALHEUREUX.   Say yee?

FREEVILL.   Let colder eld the strongst objections moove.

MALHEUREUX.   Howe's this?

FREEVILL.   No love's without some lust,
No life without some love,   160
go your wayes for an Apostata, I beleve my cast garment must be
let out in the seames for you when all is done,
„Of all the fooles that would all man out-thrust,
„He that 'gainst Nature would seeme wise is worst.

Exeunt.

ACT II

SCENE I

Enter FREEVILL, PAGES *with torches, and*
GENTLEMEN *with musicke.*

FREEVILL.   The morne is yet but younge: here gentlemen,
This is my *Beatrice* window, this the chamber
Of my betrothed dearest, whose chaste eyes,
Full of lov'd sweetnesse, and cleare cherefulnes,

143 eld] Q^c; field Q^u.   157 strongst] Q^c; straight Q^u.

Have gag'd my soule to her in joyings,   5
Shredding away all those weake under-braunches,
Of base affections, and unfruitfull heates,
Here bestow your musick to my voyce.

                                                   Cantat.
Enter BEATRICE *above.*

Alwaies a vertuous name to my chast love.
BEATRICE.   Lov'd sir the honor of your wish returne to you.   10
I cannot with a mistres complement
Forced discourses, or nice art of wit,
Give entertaine to your deere wished presence,
But safely thus, what harty gratefulnes,
Unsulleine Silence, unaffected modesty,   15
And an unignorant shamefastnes can expresse,
Receive as your protested due. Faith my hart,
I am your servant,
O let not my secure simplicity, breed your mislike,
As one quite voyde of skill,   20
Tis Grace inough in us not to be ill.
I can some good, and faith I mean no hurt,
Do not then sweete wrong sober ignorance,
I judge you all of vertue, and our vowes,
Should kill all feares that base distrust can moove.   25
My soule what say you, still you love?
FREEVILL.   Still? My vowe is up above me, and like time
Irrevocable. I am sworne all yours,
No beauty shall untwine our armes, no face
In my eyes can or shall seeme faire,   30
And would to God only to me you might
Seeme only faire; let others disesteeme
Your matchles graces: so might I safer seeme.
Envie I covet not: far, far be all ostent,
Vaine boasts of beauties: soft joyes and the rest,   35
,,He that is wise, pants, on a private brest.
So could I live in desart most unknowne,
Your selfe to me enough were Populous,
Your eyes shall be my joyes, my wine that still

17 protested] Q^c; pretested Q^u.   36 pants] Q^c; pant Q^u.

Shall drowne my often cares, your onely voyce   40
Shall cast a slumber on my listning sence,
You with soft lip shall onely ope mine eyes,
And sucke theire lidds a sunder, onely you
Shall make me wish to live, and not feare death,
So on your cheekes I might yeild latest breath,   45
O he that thus may live, and thus shall dye,
May well be envied of a dietie.

BEATRICE.   Deare my lov'd hart be not so passionate, nothing
extreame lives long.

FREEVILL.   „But not to be extreame? Nothing in love's extreame   50
my love receives no meane.

BEATRICE.   I give you fayth, and pre thee since poore soule I am
so easy to beleeve thee, make it much more pitty to deceive me.
Weare this sleight favor in my remembrance.

Throweth downe a ring to him.

FREEVILL.   Which when I part from, hope the best of life, ever   55
part from me.

BEATRICE.   I take you and your word, which may ever live your
servant. See day is quite broke up, the best of houres.

FREEVILL.   Good morrow gracefull mistres, our nuptiall day
holds.   60

BEATRICE.   With happy constancy a wished day.

Exit.

Enter MALHEUREUX.

FREEVILL.   My selfe and all content rest with you.

MALHEUREUX.   The studious morne with paler cheeke drawes on,
The dayes bold light. Harke how the free-borne birdes
Caroll their unaffected passions,   65

The Nitingalls sing.

Now sing they sonnets, thus they crye, we love.
O breath of heaven! Thus they harmles soules
Give intertaine to mutuall affects.
They have no Baudes: no mercenary bedds

46 he that thus] Q^e; that he this Q^u.
50 extreame? Nothing] extreame, nothing Q.

No politike restraints: no artificiall heats   70
No faint dissemblings, no custome makes them blush,
No shame afflicts theire name. O you happy beastes
In whome an inborne heat is not held sinne,
How far transcend you wretched, wretched man
Whome nationall custome, Tyrannous respects   75
Of slavish order, fetters: lames his power
Calling that sinne in us, which in all things els
Is natures highest vertue. *O miseri quorum gaudia crimen habent.*
Sure nature against vertue crosse doth fall
Or vertues selfe is oft unnaturall.   80
That I should love a strumpet I a man of Snowe.
Now shame forsake me! Whether am I fallen!
A creature of a publique use, my frendes love to!
To live to be a talke to men, a shame
To my professed vertue.   ,,O accursed reason,   85
,,How many eyes hast thou to see thy shame
,,And yet how blind one's to prevent defame!

FREEVILL. *Diaboli virtus in Lumbis est,* morrow my frend: come,
I could make a tedious scene of this now but, what, pah, thou art
in love with a Courtezan, why sir, should we loath all strumpets? 90
Sume men should hate their owne mothers or sisters, a sinne
against kinde I can tell you.

MALHEUREUX. May it beseeme a wise man to be in love?

FREEVILL. Let wise men alone, twill beseeme thee and me well
enough.   95

MALHEUREUX. Shall I not offend the vowe band of our frend-
ship?

FREEVILL. What to affect that which thy frend affected? By
heaven I resigne her freely, the creature and I must growe of.
By this time shee has assurely heard of my resolved marriage,   100
and no question sweares, Gods Sacrament, ten Towsand Divells.
Ile resigne Ifaith.

MALHEUREUX. I would but imbrace her, heare her speake, and
at the most but kisse her.

FREEVILL. O frend he that could live with the smoake of roast 105
meate might live at a cheape rate.

MALHEUREUX. I shall neere proove hartely receaved,

78 *gaudia*] *gaud.a* Q.   87 one's] once Q.

A kinde of flat ungratious modesty,
An insufficient dulnes staines my haviour.

FREEVILL.   No matter sir, In-sufficiency and sottishnes are much   110
commendable in a most discommendable action, now could I
swallow thee, and thou hadst wont to be so harsh and cold, ile tell
thee. Hell and the prodegies of angrie Jove are not so fearefull
to a thinking minde as a man without affection. Why frend, Phi-
losophie and nature are all one, love is the center in which all lines   115
close the common bonde of being.

MALHEUREUX.   O but a chast reserved privatnes, a modest continence.

FREEVILL.   Ile tell thee what, take this as firmest sence,
„Incontinence will force a Continence,   120
„Heate wasteth heate, light defaceth light,
„Nothing is spoyled but by his proper might.
This is some thing too waighty for thy floore.

MALHEUREUX.   But how so ere you shade it, the worlds eye
Shines hot and open ont,   125
Lying, malice, envie, are held but slidyngs,
Errors of rage, when custome and the world
Calls lust a crime spotted with blackest terrors.

FREEVILL.   Where errors are held Crimes, Crimes are but errors.
Along sir to her shee is an arrand strumpet: and a strumpet is   130
A Sarpego: Venomde Gonory to man
Things actually possessed:

                    Offer to go out and suddenly draws backe.

                    yet since thou art in love
And againe as good make use of a Statue,
A body without a soule, a carkasse three monethes dead,
Yet since thou art in love.   135

MALHEUREUX.   Death man, my destiny I cannot choose.

FREEVILL.   Nay I hope so, againe they sell but onely flesh,
No jot affection, so that even in the enjoying,
Absentem marmoreamque putes, yet since you needs must love.

MALHEUREUX.   Unavoidable though folly, worse then madnes.   140

FREEVILL.   Its true, but since you needs must love, you must
                                        know this,
He that must love, a foole, and he must kisse.

Enter COCLEDEMOY.

M. *Cocledemoy ut vales Domine!*

COCLEDEMOY.   *Ago tibi gratias,* my worshipfull friend, how
do'es your friend?   145

FREEVILL.   Out you rascall.

COCLEDEMOY.   Hang toastes, you are an Asse, much a your
worships brayne lyes in your Calves, bread a God boy, I was at
supper last night with a new weande bulchin, bread a God,
drunke, horribly drunke, horribly drunke, there was a wench   150
one *Franke Frailty,* a puncke, an honest pole-cat, of a cleane
In-step, sound legge, smooth thigh, and the nimble Divell in her
buttocke, ah fiest a grace! When saw you *Tysefew,* or M.
Caqueteur, that pratling gallant of a good draught, common
customes, fortunate, impudence and sound fart.   155

FREEVILL.   Away Rogue.

COCLEDEMOY.   Hang toastes, my fine boy, my companions are
worshipfull.

MALHEUREUX.   Yes I heare you are taken up with schollers
and church men.   160

Enter HOLIFERNES *the Barbar.*

COCLEDEMOY.   *Quanquam te Marce fili* my boy, does your worship want a Barbar Surgeon?

FREEVILL.   Farewell knave, beware the *Mulligrubs.*

Exeunt FREEVILL *and* MALHEUREUX.

COCLEDEMOY.   Let the *Mulligrubs* beware the knave! What a
Barbar Surgeon, my delicate boy?   165

HOLIFERNES.   Yes sir an apprentise to surgery.

⟨COCLEDEMOY.⟩   Ti's my fine boy, to what bawdy house doth
your Maister belong? Whats thy name?

HOLIFERNES.   *Holifernes Rains-cure.*

COCLEDEMOY.   *Rains-cure?* Good M. *Holifernes* I desire your   170
further acquaintance, nay pray yee bee covered my fine boy, kill
thy itch and heale thy skabes, is thy Maister rotten?

HOLIFERNES.   My father forsooth is dead.

157 companions are] Q^c; companion as Q^u.   163 Farewell] Barewell Q.

COCLEDEMOY.   And laid in his grave, alas what comfort shall
Peggy then have.   175

HOLIFERNES.   None but me sir, thats my mothers sonne I assure
you.

COCLEDEMOY.   Mothers sonne, a good witty boy, would live to
read an Homilie well. And to whome are you going now?

HOLIFERNES.   Marry forsooth to trim M. *Mulligrub* the Vintner.   180

COCLEDEMOY.   Doe you know M. *Mulligrub?*

HOLIFERNES.   My Godfather Sir.

COCLEDEMOY.   Good boy hold up thy chops, I pray thee doe
one thing for me, my name is *Gudgeon.*

HOLIFERNES.   Good M. *Gudgeon.*   185

COCLEDEMOY.   Lend me thy bason, razer, and Apron.

HOLIFERNES.   O Lord sir.

COCLEDEMOY.   Wel spoken, good english, but whats thy furniture worth?

HOLIFERNES.   O Lord sir I know not.   190

COCLEDEMOY.   Well spoken, a boy of a good wit, holde this
pawne, where dost dwell?

HOLIFERNES.   At the signe of the three razers sir.

COCLEDEMOY.   A signe of good shaving my catastrophonicall
fine boy, I have an odde jest to trim M. *Mulligrub* for a wager, a   195
jest boy, a humor. Ile returne thy thinges presently, hold.

HOLIFERNES.   What meane you good M. *Gudgeon?*

COCLEDEMOY.   Nothing faith but a jest boy, drinke that, Ile
recoile presently.

HOLIFERNES.   You'le not stay long?   200

COCLEDEMOY.   As I am an honest man. The 3. razers?

HOLIFERNES.   I sir.

Exit Holifernes.

COCLEDEMOY.   Good, and if I shave not M. *Mulligrub*, my wit
has no edge, and I may goe cacke in my pewter. Let me see, a
Barbar, my scurvie tongue will discover me, must dissemble,   205
must disguise. For my beard, my false hayre, for my tongue,
Spanish, Dutch, or Welsh, no, a Northerne Barbar, very good,
widdow *Raines-cures* man well. Newly entertainde, right, so,
hang tostes, all cardes have white backes, and all knaves would

seeme to have white breastes, so proceede, now worshipfull 210
Cocledemoy.

Exit COCLEDEMOY *in his Barbars furniture.*

⟨SCENE II⟩

Enter MARY FAUGH, *and* FRANCISCHINA *with her*
Hayre Loose, chasing.

MARY FAUGH.   Nay good sweete daughter, doe not swagger so,
you heare your love is to bee married, true, he does cast you off,
right he will leave you to the world, what then? Tho blew and
white, black and greene leave you, may not redde and yellow
entertain you, is there but one coullor in the Raine-bow?   5
FRANCISCHINA.   *Grand Grincome* on your sentences, Gods
sacrament, ten towsand divels take you, you ha brought mine
love, mine honor, mine boddy all to noting.
MARY FAUGH.   To nothing! I'le be sworne I have brought
them to all the thinges I could, I ha made as much a your   10
maydenhead, and you had beene mine owne daughter! I could
not ha sold your Mayden head oftner then I ha done! I ha sworn
for you God forgive me! I have made you acquainted with the
Spaniard *Don Skirtoll*, with the Italian, M. *Beieroane*, with the
Irish Lord, S. *Patrick*, with the Dutch Marchant, *Haunce Herkin*   15
Glukin Skellam Flappdragon, and specially with the greatest
French, and now lastly with this English (yet in my conscience)
an honest Gentleman: and am I now growne one of the accursed
with you for my labour? Is this my reward, am I calde Bawde?
Well *Mary Faugh*, goe thy wayes *Mary Faugh*, thy kind heart will   20
bring thee to the Hospitall.
FRANCISCHINA.   Nay good Naunt, you'le helpe me to an oder
love, vil you not?
MARY FAUGH.   Out thou naughty belly, wouldst thou make mee
thy Bawde? Thu'st best make me thy Bawde, I ha kept counsell   25
for thee. Who paide the Apothecary, wast not honest *Mary*
Faugh? Who redeemde thy petticote and mantle, wast not honest
Mary Faugh? Who helped thee to thy custome not of swaggering
Ireland Captaines, nor of 2.s. Innes a court men, but with honest

II. II. S.D. *Hayre*ᴧ] *Harye*, Q.

flatte-cappes, wealthy flat-caps, that pay for their pleasure the   30
best of any men in Europe, nay, which is more in *London*, and
dost thou defie me vile creature?

FRANCISCHINA.   *Foutra* pon you Vitch, Bawde, Pole-catte,
Paugh, did not you prayse *Freevill* to mine love?

MARY FAUGH.   I did prayse I confesse, I did prayse him, I sede   35
hee was a foole, an unthrift, a true whoremaister, I confesse, a
constant drabbe keeper I confesse, but what the winde is turnde.

FRANCISCHINA.   It is, it is vile woman, reprobate woman,
naughtie woman it is, vat sal become of mine poore flesh now?
Mine boddy must turne Turke for 2.d. O *Divela*, life a mine art,   40
Ick sall be revengde, doe ten thousand Hell damme me, Ick
sal have the rogue trote cut, and his love, and his friend, and all
his affinitie sall smart, sall dye, sal hang, now legion of devill
seaze him, de gran pest, S. *Anthonies* fire, and de hot Neopolitan
poc rotte him.   45

Enter FREEVILL *and* MALHEUREUX.

FREEVILL.   *Francischina*.

FRANCISCHINA.   O mine seete, deerst, kindest, mine loving, O
mine towsand, ten towsand, delicated, petty seet art a mine a
deere leevest affection.

FREEVILL.   Why Monky, no fashion in you? Give entertaine to   50
my friend.

FRANCISCHINA.   Icke sal make de most of you, dat curtesie may:
Aunt *Mary*, Mettre *Faugh*, stooles, stooles for des gallantes.

Cantat Gallice

Mine Mettre sing non oder song,
    Frolique, frolique Sir,   55
But still complaine me doe her wrong,
    Lighten your heart Sir,
For me did but kisse her,
For me did but kis her,
    And so let go.   60

Your friend is very heavy, ick sall neere like such sad company.

FREEVILL.   No thou delightest onely in light Company.

30 flatte-] HALLIWELL; atte- Q.   42 rogue] rouge Q.
53 S.D. *Cantat Gallice*] *follows* l. 48 *in* Q.
54–60 *Run on in* Q (Lineation, but not arrangement, as WINE).

FRANCISCHINA.   By mine trot, he been very sad, vat ayle you sir.

MALHEUREUX.   A tooth ake Lady, a paultry rheume.

FRANCISCHINA.   De diet is very goot for de rheume.   65

FREEVILL.   How far of dwels the house surgeon *Mary Faugh*?

MARY FAUGH.   You are a prophane fellow I faith, I little thought
to heare such ungodly termes come from your lips.

FRANCISCHINA.   Pre de now, tis but a toy, a very trifle.

FREEVILL.   I care not for the valew, *Franke*, but I faith—   70

FRANCISCHINA.   I fait, me must needes have it (dis is *Beatrice*
ring, oh could I get it,) seet pree de now, as ever you have em-
braced me with a hearty arme, a warme thought, or a pleasing
touch, as ever you will professe to love me, as ever you do wish
me life, give me dis ring, dis litle ring.   75

FREEVILL.   Pree thee but not uncivillie importunate, sha not ha't,
faith I care not for thee, nor thy jelousie, sha not ha't ifaith.

FRANCISCHINA.   You doe not love me, I heare of Sir *Hubert
Subboys* daughter Mistresse *Beatrice*, Gods Sacrament, ick could
scratch out her eyes, and sucke the holes.   80

FREEVILL.   Goe y'are growne a puncke rampant.

FRANCISCHINA.   So get thee gone, nere more behold min eyes
by thee made wretched.

FREEVILL.   *Mary Faugh* farewell, farewell *Franck*.

FRANCISCHINA.   Sall I not ha de ring?   85

FREEVILL.   No by the Lord.

FRANCISCHINA.   By te Lord?

FREEVILL.   By the Lord.

FRANCISCHINA.   Goe to your new Blouze, your unprovde
sluttery, your modest Mettre forsooth.   90

FREEVILL.   Marry will I forsooth.

FRANCISCHINA.   Will you marry forsooth?

FREEVILL.   Doe not turne witch before thy time.

⟨FRANCISCHINA.⟩   With all my hart. Sir, you will stay?

MALHEUREUX.   I am no whit my selfe, *Video meliora proboque*,   95
But raging lust my fate all strong doth move:
„The Gods themselves cannot be wise and love.

FREEVILL.   Your wishes to you.

Exit FREEVILL.

89 unprovde] BULLEN; unproude Q.
94 FRANCISCHINA.] *spoken by Freevill in* Q.

MALHEUREUX. Beautie entirely choyce.

FRANCISCHINA. Pray yee prove a man of fashion, and neglect 100
the neglected.

MALHEUREUX. Can such a raritie bee neglected, can there be
measurd or sinne in loving such a creature?

FRANCISCHINA. O min poore forsaken hart.

MALHEUREUX. I can not containe, he saw thee not that left thee, 105
If there be wisedome, reason, honor, grace
Or any foolishly esteemed vertue,
In giving o're possession of such beautie,
Let me be vitious, so I may be lov'de,
Passion I am thy slave, sweete it shall be my grace,   110
That I account thy love, my onely vertue:
Shall I sweare I am thy most vowed servant.

FRANCISCHINA. Mine vowed, go, go, go, I can no more of love,
no, no, no, you bin all unconstant, O unfaithfull men, tyrantes,
betrayers, de very enjoying us, looseth us, and when you onely 115
ha made us hatefull, you onely hate us: O mine forsaken hart.

MALHEUREUX. I must not rave, Scilence and modesty two
customarie vertues: will you be my mistresse?

FRANCISCHINA. Mettres? Ha, ha, ha.

MALHEUREUX. Will you lie with me?   120

FRANCISCHINA. Lie with you? O no, you men will out-lie any
woman, fait me no more can love.

MALHEUREUX. No matter, let me enjoy your bed.

FRANCISCHINA. O vile man, vat do you tinck on me, doe you
take mee to be a beast, a creature that for sence onely will enter- 125
taine love, and not onely for love, love? O brutish abhomination!

MALHEUREUX. Why then I pray thee love, and with thy love
enjoy me.

FRANCISCHINA. Give me reason to affect you, will you sweare
you love me?   130

MALHEUREUX. So seriously, that I protest no office so dan-
gerous, no deede so unreasonable, no cost so heavie, but I vow to
the utmost tentation of my best being to effect it.

FRANCISCHINA. Sall I, or can I trust againe? O foole,
Now naturall tis for us to be abusde!   135
Sall ick be sure that no satietie,

107 Or] 1633; Of Q.

No inoying, not time shall languish your affection?
MALHEUREUX.   If there be ought in brayne, hart or hand,
  Can make you doubtlesse, I am your vowed servant.
FRANCISCHINA.   Will you doe one ting for me?   140
MALHEUREUX.   Can I doe it?
FRANCISCHINA.   Yes, yes, but ick doe not love dis same *Freevill.*
MALHEUREUX.   Well?
FRANCISCHINA.   Nay I do hate him.
MALHEUREUX.   So?   145
FRANCISCHINA.   By this kisse I hate him.
MALHEUREUX.   I love to feele such othes, sweare againe.
FRANCISCHINA.   No, no, did you ever heare of any that lovde
  at the first sight?
MALHEUREUX.   A thing most proper.   150
FRANCISCHINA.   Now fait, I judge it all incredible, untill this
  houre I saw you pritty fayre eyed yout, would you enjoy me?
MALHEUREUX.   Rather then my breath, even as my being.
FRANCISCHINA.   Vel, had ick not made a vow.
MALHEUREUX.   What vow?   155
FRANCISCHINA.   O let me forget it, it makes us both despaire.
MALHEUREUX.   Deare soule what vow?
FRANCISCHINA.   Hah, good morrow gentle Sir, endevour to
  forget me, as I must be enforced to forget all men. Sweet mind
  rest in you.   160
MALHEUREUX.   Stay, let not my desire burst me, O my impatient
  heate endures no resistance, no protraction, there is no being for
  me but your suddaine injoying.
FRANCISCHINA.   I doe not love *Freevill.*
MALHEUREUX.   But what vow, what vow?   165
FRANCISCHINA.   So long as *Freevill* lives, I must not love.
MALHEUREUX.   Then he.
FRANCISCHINA.   Must.
MALHEUREUX.   Die.
FRANCISCHINA.   I, no there is no such vehemence in your   170
  affectes. Would I were any thing, so he were not.
MALHEUREUX.   Will you be mine when he is not?
FRANCISCHINA.   Will I? Deare, deare breast, by this most zealous
  kisse, but I will not perswade you: but if you hate him that I loath
  most deadly, yet as you please, i'le perswade noting.   175

MALHEUREUX.   Will you be onely mine.

FRANCISCHINA.   Vill I? How hard tis for true love to dissemble,
I am onely yours.

MALHEUREUX.   Tis as irrevocable as breath, he dyes. Your love.

FRANCISCHINA.   My vow, not untill hee be dead,   180
Which that I may be sure not to infringe,
Dis token of his death, sall satisfie,
He has a ring, as deare as the ayre to him,
His new loves gift: tat got and brought to me,
I shall assured your possessed rest.   185

MALHEUREUX.   To kill a man?

FRANCISCHINA.   O done safely, a quarrell suddain pickt, with
an advantage strike, then bribe, a little coyne, al's safe, deare
soule, but Ile not set you on.

MALHEUREUX.   Nay hee is gone, the ring, well, come, little 190
more liberall of thy love.

FRANCISCHINA.   Not yet my vow.

MALHEUREUX.   O heaven, there is no hell but loves prolongings,
deare farewell.

FRANCISCHINA.   Farewell. ⟨*Aside*⟩ Now does my hart swell
high, for my revenge 195
Has birth and forme, first friend sal kill his friend,
He dat survives, i'le hang, besides de
Chast *Beatrice* ile vexe: onely de ring.
Dat got the world sall know the worst of evils.
„Woman corrupted is the worst of devils.   200

FRANCISCHINA ⟨*and* MARY FAUGH⟩ *Exeunt.*

MALHEUREUX.   To kill my friend! O tis to kill my selfe,
Yet mans but mans excrement, man breeding man,
As he do's wormes ⟨*He spits.*⟩ or this, to spoile this nothing.
The body of a man is of the selfe same soile,
As Oxe or horse, no murther to kill these,   205
As for that onely part, which makes us man,
Murther wants power to toucht: O wit how vile,
How hellish art thou, when thou raisest nature
Gainst sacred faith! Thinke more to kill a friend
To gaine a woman, to loose a vertuous selfe,   210

204 soile] WALLEY AND WILSON; soule Q.

For appetite and sensual end, whose very having,
Looseth all appetite, and gives satietie,
That corporall end, remorse and inward blushinges,
Forcing us loath the steame of our owne heates,
Whilste friendship closde in vertue being spiritual,   215
Tastes no such languishinges and moments pleasure,
With much repentance, but like rivers flow,
And further that they runne, they bigger grow.
Lord how was I misgone, how easie ti's to erre,
When passion wil not give us leave to thinke?   220
„A learn'd that is an honest man may feare
„And lust, and rage, and malice, and any thing,
„When he is taken uncollected suddenly:
„Ti's sinne of colde blood, mischiefe with wak'd eyes;
„That is the damned and the truely vice,   225
„Not he that's passionles but he 'bove passion's wise.
My friend shall know it all.

                                                            Exit

                            ⟨SCENE III⟩

        Enter Maister MULLIGRUB, *and Mistresse* MULLIGRUB,
                    shee with bag of money.

MRS MULLIGRUB.   It is right I assure you, just fifteene pounds.
MULLIGRUB.   Well *Cocledemoy* tis thou putst me to this charge,
    but and I catch thee, I'le charge thee with as many irons: well, is
    the Barbar come, ile be trimd and then to Cheapeside, to buy a
    faire peece of plate, to furnish the losse, is the Barbar come?   5
MRS MULLIGRUB.   Truth husband, surely heaven is not pleasde
    with our vocation; we do winke at the sinnes of our people, our
    wines are Protestantes, and I speake it to my griefe, and to the
    burthen of my conscience, we frie our fish with salt butter.

                                                            Exit

MULLIGRUB.   Goe looke to your busines, mend the matter and   10
    skore false with a vengeance.

Enter COCLEDEMOY *like a Barbar.*

    Welcome friend, whose man?

        II. III. S.D. *bag*] Q^c; *a bag* Q^u.   8 wines] Q^c; wiues Q^u.

COCLEDEMOY.   Widdow *Raines-cures* man, and shall please your
good worship, my names *Andrew Sharke.*

MULLIGRUB.   How do's my God-sonne good *Andrew?*   15

COCLEDEMOY.   Very well, hee's gone to trim M. *Quicquid* our
Parson. Hold up your head.

MULLIGRUB.   How long have you beene a Barbar *Andrew?*

COCLEDEMOY.   Not long Sir, this two yeare.

MULLIGRUB.   What and a good worke man already, I dare scarse   20
trust my heade to thee.

COCLEDEMOY.   O feare not, we ha polde better men then you, we
learn the trade very quickly. Will your good worship be shaven
or cut?

MULLIGRUB.   As you will. What trade didst live by, before thou   25
turnedst Barbar *Andrew?*

COCLEDEMOY.   I was a Pedler in Germany, but my countrimen
thrive better by this trade.

MULLIGRUB.   Wha's the newes Barbar, thou art sometimes at
Court.   30

COCLEDEMOY.   Sometimes pole a Page or so sir.

MULLIGRUB.   And what's the newes? How doe all my good
Lordes and all my good Ladies, and all the rest of my acquaintance.

COCLEDEMOY ⟨*aside*⟩.   What an arrogant knave's this, Ile   35
acquaintance yee (tis cash). Say yee sir.

Hee spieth the bag

MULLIGRUB.   And what newes? What newes? Good *Andrew.*

COCLEDEMOY.   Marry sir you know the Conduit at Greenwich,
and the under-holes that spowtes up water.

MULLIGRUB.   Very well, I was washt there one day, and so was   40
my wife, you might have wrung her smocke ifaith, but what a
those holes?

COCLEDEMOY.   Thus Sir, out of those little holes in the midst of
the night crawlde out 24. huge horrible, monstrous, fearefull
devouring.   45

MULLIGRUB.   Blesse us.

COCLEDEMOY.   Serpents, which no sooner were beheld, but they
turnd to mastives which howlde, those mastives instantly turnde

———————————

36 (tis cash).] tis cash, Qᵘ; (tis cash,) Qᶜ.

to Cockes which crowed, those cockes in a moment were
changde to Beares which roard, which Beares are at this hower   50
to bee yet seene in *Paris Garden*, living upon nothing but
toasted cheese and greene onions.

MULLIGRUB.   By the Lord and this may be: my wife and I will
go see them, this portends something.

COCLEDEMOY.   Yes worshipfull. ⟨*aside*⟩ Fiest, thou'st feele what   55
portendes by and by.

MULLIGRUB.   And what more newes? You shave the worlde,
especially you Barbar Surgeons you know the ground of many
thinges, you are cunning privie searchers, by the mas you
skowre all: what more newes?   60

COCLEDEMOY.   They say Sir that 25. coople of Spanish Jennetes
are to bee seene hand in hand daunce the olde measures, whilest
six goodly Flaunders Mares play to them on a noyse of
flutes.

MULLIGRUB.   O monstrous! This is a lie a my word, nay and this   65
bee not a lie, I am no foole I warrant, nay make an Asse of mee
once?

COCLEDEMOY.   Shut your eyes close, wincke sure sir, this bal wil
make you smart.

MULLIGRUB.   I do winke.   70

COCLEDEMOY.   Your head will take cold.

COCLEDEMOY puts on a Coxecombe on
MULLIGRUBS head.

I will put on your good worships night-cap, whilest I shave you.
⟨*aside*⟩ So, mum: hang toastes: faugh: viah: sparrowes must
pecke and *Cocledemoy* munch.

⟨*Exit* COCLEDEMOY.⟩

MULLIGRUB.   Ha, ha, ha, 25. couple of Spanish Jennets to daunce   75
the olde measures. *Andrew*, makes my worshippe laugh, ifaith,
dost take me for an Asse *Andrew*? Dost know one *Cocledemoy* in
towne? He made mee an Asse last night, but ile asse him. Art
thou free *Andrew*? Shave me well, I shall bee one of the common
Councell shortly, and then *Andrew*, why *Andrew*, *Andrew*, doest   80
leave me in the Suddes?

Cantat.

56 portendes] Q^c; pertendes Q^u.   66 make] Q^c; mafle Q^u.

Why *Andrew* I shall be blinde with winking. Ha *Andrew*, wife,
Andrew, what meanes this, wife, my money wife.

Enter MRS MULLIGRUB.

MRS MULLIGRUB.   What's the noyse with you? What ails you?
MULLIGRUB.   Wheres the Barbar?   85
MRS MULLIGRUB.   Gone, I saw him depart long since, why are
not you trimd?
MULLIGRUB.   Trimd, O wife, I am shav'd, did you take hence the
money?
MRS MULLIGRUB.   I toucht it not as I am Religious.   90
MULLIGRUB.   O Lord I have winkt faire.

Enter HOLIFERNES.

HOLIFERNES.   I pray Godfather give me your blessing.
MULLIGRUB.   O *Holifernes*, O wheres thy mothers *Andrew?*
HOLIFERNES.   Blessing Godfather.
MULLIGRUB.   The divell choake thee, where's *Andrew* thy   95
mothers man?
HOLIFERNES.   My mother hath none such forsooth.
MULLIGRUB.   My money, 15.l. Plague of all *Andrews*, who wast
trimd me?
HOLIFERNES.   I know not Godfather, onelie one mette me, as I 100
was comming to you, and borrowed my furniture, as he saide for
a jest sake.
MULLIGRUB.   What kinde of fellow?
HOLIFERNES.   A thick elderly stub-bearded fellow.
MULLIGRUB.   *Cocledemoy, Cocledemoy*, raise all the Wise men in 105
the streete, Ile hang him with my owne hands: O wife, some *Rosa
Solis*.
MRS MULLIGRUB.   Good husband take comfort in the Lord, Ile
play the Divell, but ile recover it, have a good conscience ti's but a
weekes cutting in the Terme.   110
MULLIGRUB.   O wife, O wife, O *Jacke* how does thy mother?
Is there any Fidlers in the house?
MRS MULLIGRUB.   Yes, M. *Creakes* noyse.
MULLIGRUB.   Bid 'em play, laugh, make merry, cast up my ac-
countes, for ile go hang my selfe presently, I will not curse, but a 115
poxe on *Cocledemoy*, he has polde and shavde me, he has trimd
me.   *Exeunt.*

ACT III

SCENE I

Enter BEATRICE, CRISPINELLA, *and Nurs* PUTIFER.

PUTIFER. Nay good child, A love once more, M. *Freevills Sonnet*,
a the kisse you gave him.

BEATRICE. Sha'te good Nurse,
    Purest lips soft banks of blisses
    Selfe alone, deserving kisses: 5
    O give me leave to, etc.

CRISPINELLA. Pish sister *Beatrice*, pree thee reade no more,
my stomacke alate stands against kissing extreamly.

BEATRICE. Why good *Crispinella*?

CRISPINELLA. By the faith, and trust I beare to my face, tis   10
grown one of the most unsavorie Ceremonies: Boddy a beautie,
tis one of the most unpleasing injurious customes to Ladyes: any
fellow that has but one nose on his face, and standing collor and
skirtes also linde with Taffety sarcenet, must salute us on the lipps
as familierly: Soft skins save us, there was a stubbearded John a   15
stile with a ploydens face saluted me last day, and stroke his
bristles through my lippes, I ha spent 10. shillings in *pomatum*
since to skinne them againe. Marry if a nobleman or a knight with
one locke vissit us, though his uncleane goose turd greene teeth
ha the palsy, his nostrells smell worse then a putrified maribone,   20
and his loose beard drops into our bosome, yet wee must kisse him
with a cursy, a curse, for my part I had as live they would break
wynd in my lipps.

BEATRICE. Fy *Crispinella* you speake too broad.

CRISPINELLA. No jot sister, lets neere be ashamed to speake   25
what we be not ashamd to thinke, I dare as boldly speake venery,
as think venery.

BEATRICE. Faith sister ile begone if you speake so broad.

III. I. 19 turd] 1633; turnd Q.

CRISPINELLA. Will you so? Now bashfulnes seaz you, we
pronounce boldly Robbery, Murder, treason, which deedes must   30
needes be far more lothsome then an act which is so naturall, just
and necessary, as that of procreation, you shall have an hipo-
criticall vestall virgin speake, that with close teeth publikely,
which she will receive with open mouth privately. For my owne
part I consider nature without apparell, without disguising of   35
custome or complement. I give thoughts wordes, and wordes
truth, and truth boldnes, she whose honest freenes makes it her
vertue, to speake what she thinks, will make it her necessity to
thinke what is good. I love no prohibited things, and yet I would
have nothing prohibited by policy but by vertue, for as in the   40
fashion of time, those bookes that are cald in, are most in sale and
request, so in nature those actions that are most prohibited, are
most desired.

BEATRICE. Good quick sister, stay your pace we are privat, but
the world would censure you, for truly severe modesty is womens   45
vertue.

CRISPINELLA. Fye, Fye, vertue is a free pleasant buxom
qualitie: I love a constant countenance well, but this froward
ignorant coynes, sower austere lumpish uncivill privatenes, that
promises nothing but rough skins, and hard stooles, ha, fy ont   50
good for nothing but for nothing. Well nurse, and what do you
conceave of all this?

PUTIFER. Nay faith my conceaving dayes be done, marry for
kissing ile defend that, thats within my compas, but for my own
part heers mistres *Beatrice* is to be married with the gracc of God,   55
a fine gentleman he is shall have her and I warrant a stronge, he
has a legg like a post, a nose like a Lion, a brow like a Bull, and
a beard of most faire expectation: this weeke you must marry
him, and I now will read a lecture to you both, how you shall
behave your selves to your husbands, the first monneth of your   60
nuptiall, I ha broake my skull about it, I can tell you and there is
much braine in it.

CRISPINELLA. Read it to my sister good nurse, for I assure
you ile nere marry.

PUTIFER. Marry God forfend, what will you doe then?   65

CRISPINELLA. Fayth strive against the flesh. Marry? No fayth,
husbands are like lotts in the lottery: you may drawe forty blankes

before you find one that has any prise in him. A husband generally
is a careles dominering thing that growes like coroll which as long
as it is under water is soft and tender, but as soone as it has got   70
his branch above the waves is presently hard stiffe, not to be
bowed but burst, so when your husband is a sutor and under
your choyse, Lord how suple hee is, how obsequious, how at
your service sweet Lady: once married, got up his head above,
a stiffe crooked knobby inflexible tyrannous creature he grows   75
then they turne like water, more you would imbrace the lesse
you hould. Ile live my owne woman, and if the worst come to
the worst, I had rather proove a wagge then a foole.
BEATRICE.   O but a vertuous marriage.
CRISPINELLA.   Vertuous marrige? There is no more affinity   80
betwixt vertue and marriage, then betwixt a man and his horse,
indeed vertue getts up uppon marriage sometimes, and manageth
it in the right way, but marriage is of another peece, for as a horse
may be without a man, and a man without a horse, so marriage
you know is often without vertue, and vertue I am sure more oft   85
without marriage. But thy match sister, by my troth I thinke
twill do well, hees a well shapt cleane lipp'd gentleman of a hand-
some, but not affected finenes, a good faithfull eye, and a well
humord cheeke, would he did not stoope in the shoulders for thy
sake, see here he is.   90
Enter FREEVILL *and* TYSEFEW.

FREEVILL.   Good day Sweete.
CRISPINELLA.   Good morrow brother nay you shall have my
lip, good morrow servant.
TYSEFEW.   Good morrow sweete life.
CRISPINELLA.   Life? Dost call thy mistres life?   95
TYSEFEW.   Life, yes why not life?
CRISPINELLA.   How many mistresses hast thou?
TYSEFEW.   Some nine.
CRISPINELLA.   Why then thou hast nine lives like a Cat.
TYSEFEW.   Mew you would be taken up for that.   100
CRISPINELLA.   Nay good let me still sit, we lowe statures love
still to sit, least when we stand we may be supposed to sit.
TYSEFEW   Dost not weare high corke shooes: chopines?

CRISPINELLA. Monstrous on's. I am as many other are, peec'd
above and peec'd beneath.   105

TYSEFEW. Still the best part in the,

CRISPINELLA. And yet all will scarce make me so high as one of
the Gyants stilts that stalkes before my Lord Maiors pageant.

TYSEFEW. By the Lord so I thought 'twas for some thing
Mistres *Joyce* jested at thy high insteps.   110

CRISPINELLA. She might well inough, and long inough, before
I would be ashamed of my shortnes, what I made or can mend
my selfe I may blush at; but what nature put upon me, let her be
ashamed for me, I ha nothing to doe with it, I forget my beauty.

TYSEFEW. Fayth *Joyce* is a foolish bitter creature.   115

CRISPINELLA. A pretty mildewed wench she is.

TYSEFEW. And faire.

CRISPINELLA. As my selfe.

TYSEFEW. O you forget your beauty now.

CRISPINELLA. Troth I never remember my beauty, but as some   120
men doe religion for controversies sake,

BEATRICE. A motion sister.

CRISPINELLA. Ninivie, Julius Caesar, Jonas, or the distruction
of Jerusalem.

BEATRICE. My love heere.   125

CRISPINELLA. Pree thee call him not love, 'tis the drabs phrase,
nor sweete honie, nor my cunny, nor deare duckling, 'tis the
Cittizen termes, but call me him.

BEATRICE. What?

CRISPINELLA. Anithing, what'st the motion?   130

BEATRICE. You know this night our parents have intended
solemnly to contract us, and my Love to grace the feast hath
promised a maske.

FREEVILL. You'le make one *Tysefew*, and *Caqueteur* shall fill up a
rome.   135

TYSEFEW. Fore heaven well remembred he borrowed a diamond
of me last night to grace his finger in your visitation: The Lying
Creature will sweare some straung thing on it now.

Enter CAQUETEUR.

CRISPINELLA. Peace, he's here, stand close, lurke.

CAQUETEUR. Good morrow most deere, and worthy to be most 140
wise, how do's my mistresse?

CRISPINELLA. Morrow sweete servant, you glister, pree thee
let's see that stone.

CAQUETEUR. A toy Lady, I bought to please my finger.

CRISPINELLA. Why I am more pretious to you, than your finger. 145

CAQUETEUR. Yes, or than all my body, I sweare.

CRISPINELLA. Why, then let it be bought to please me, come
I am no professed beggar.

CAQUETEUR. Troth Mistresse; Zoones: Forsooth, I protest.

CRISPINELLA. Nay, if you turne Protestant for such a toy. 150

CAQUETEUR. In good deed la, another time ile give you a

CRISPINELLA. Is this yours to give?

CAQUETEUR. O God, forsooth mine, quoth you, nay as for that.

CRISPINELLA. Now I remember, I ha seene this on my servant
Tysefews finger. 155

CAQUETEUR. Such another.

CRISPINELLA. Nay, I am sure this is it.

CAQUETEUR. Troth tis forsooth, the poore fellow wanted money
to pay for supper last night, and so pawned it to mee, tis a pawne
ifaith, or cloe you should have it. 160

TYSEFEW. Harke ye, Thou base lying: how dares thy impudence
hope to prosper, wer't not for the priviledge of this respected
companie, I would so bange thee.

CRISPINELLA. Come hether servant. What's the matter
betwixt you two? 165

CAQUETEUR. Nothing but (hearke you) he did me some uncivile
discourtesies last night, for which, because I should not call him
to account, hee desires to make me any satisfaction: the Coward
trembles at my verie presence, but I ha him on the hippe, ile take
the forfeit on his Ringe. 170

TYSEFEW. What's that you whisper to her?

CAQUETEUR. Nothing Sir, but satisfie her, that the Ringe was
not pawnd, but onely lent by you to grace my finger, and so
tould her I crav'd your pardon, for being too familiar, or indeed
overbould with your reputation. 175

CRISPINELLA. Yes indeede he did, he said you desired to make
him any satisfaction for an uncivill discourtesie you did him last

night, but he said he had you a the hyp and would take the forfeit
of your ring.

TYSEFEW.   How now ye base Pultrone?   180

CAQUETEUR.   Hold, hold, my mistresse speakes by contraries.

TYSEFEW.   Contraries?

CAQUETEUR.   She jests, faith onely jests.

CRISPINELLA.   Sir, Ile no more a your service, you are a childe,
Ile give you to my nurse.   185

PUTIFER.   And he come to me, I can tell you as olde as I am,
what to doe with him.

CAQUETEUR.   I offer my service forsooth.

TYSEFEW.   Why so, now every dogge has his bone to knawe on.

FREEVILL.   The Maske holds, Master *Caqueteur*.   190

CAQUETEUR.   I am ready Sir, Mistresse Ile daunce with you, neere
feare, Ile grace you.

PUTIFER.   I tell you I can my singles and my doubles and my
tricke a xxtie, my carantapace, my traverse forward, and my
falling backe yet ifaith.   195

BEATRICE.   Mine, the provision for the night is ours,
Much must be our care, till night we leave you,
I am your servant be not tirannous,
Your vertue wan me, faith my loves not lust,
Good wrong me not, my most fault is much trust.   200

FREEVILL.   Untill night onely my heart be with you. Farewell
sister.

CRISPINELLA.   Adieu brother, come on sister for these sweete
meates,

FREEVILL.   Lets meete and practise presently.   205

TYSEFEW.   Content, weele but fit our pumpes. Come ye
pernitious vermine.

Exeunt ⟨all but FREEVILL⟩.

Enter MALHEUREUX.

FREEVILL.   My friend, wished houres, what newes from Babilon?
How dos the woman of *Sinne, and naturall concupisence?*

MALHEUREUX.   The eldest child of nature nere beheld so dam'd a 210
creature.

FREEVILL.   What, *In nova fert animus mutatas dicere formas?*
Which way beares the Tyde?

MALHEUREUX. Deare loved Sir, I finde a minde courageously
vitious, may put on a desperate securitie, but can never bee blessed   215
with a firme injoying and selfe satisfaction.

FREEVILL. What passion is this, my deare *Lindabridis?*

MALHEUREUX. Tis well, we both may jest, I ha beene tempted
to your death.

FREEVILL. What is the rampant Cocatrice growne mad for the   220
losse of hir man?

MALHEUREUX. Devilishly mad.

FREEVILL. As most assured of my second love?

MALHEUREUX. Right.

FREEVILL. She would have had this ring.   225

MALHEUREUX. I, and this heart, and in true proofs you were
slaine I should bring her this ring, from which she was assured
you would not part, untill from life you parted. For which
deede, and onely for which deede, I should possesse her sweetnesse.   230

FREEVILL. O bloody villaines, nothing is defamed but by his
proper selfe, Phisitions abuse remedies, Lawyers spoyle the Lawe,
and women onely shame women. You ha vow'd my death?

MALHEUREUX. My lust, not I, before my reason would, yet I
must use her. That I a man of sence should conceive endelesse   235
pleasure in a body whose soule I know to be so hideously blacke.

FREEVILL. That a man at twentie three should cry, O sweete
pleasure, and at fortie three should sigh, O sharpe Poxe: but consider man furnished with omnipotencie and you overthrowe
him, thou must coole thy impatient appetite.   240
Ti's Fate, ti's Fate.

MALHEUREUX. I doe malign my creation that I am subject to
passion. I must injoy her.

FREEVILL. I have it. Marke. I give a maske to night
To my loves kindred, in that thou shalt goe: 245
In that we two make shew of falling out,
Give seeming challenge, instantly depart,
With some suspition to present fight.
We will be seene as going to our swordes,
And after meeting, this Ring onely lent,   250
Ile lurke in some obscure place, till rumor

235 her.That] her, that Q.

(The common Bawde to loose suspitions)
Have fayned me slaine, which (in respect my selfe
Will not bee found, and our late seeming quarrell)
Will quickly sound to all as earnest truth: 255
Then to thy wench, protest me surely dead.
Shew her this Ring, injoy her, and bloud colde
Weele laugh at folly.
MALHEUREUX. O but thinke of it.
FREEVILL. Thinke of it, come away, vertue let sleepe thy
                                                    passions, 260
„What old times held as crimes, are now but fashions.
                                                    Exeunt.

⟨SCENE II⟩

Enter Master BURNISH, *and* LIONELL: *Master* MULLIGRUB
with a standing cup in his hand, and an Obligation in the other,
COCLEDEMOY *stands at the other dore disguised like a French
Pedlar, and over-heares them.*

MULLIGRUB. I am not at this time furnished, but ther's my bond
   for your Plate.
BURNISH. Your bill had ben sufficient y'are a good man, a
   standing cup parcell guilt, of 32. ounces. 11. pound, 7.
   shillings, the first of July, good plate, good man, good day   5
   good all.
MULLIGRUB. Tis my hard fortune, I will hang the knave, no,
   first he shall halfe rot in fetters in the Dungeon, his conscience
   made despairfull, ile hyre a Knave a purpose, shal assure him he
   is damn'd, and after see him with mine owne eyes, hanged with-   10
   out singing any Psalme. Lord that hee has but one necke.
BURNISH. You are too tyrannous, you'le use me no further.
MULLIGRUB. No Sir, lend mee your servant, onely to carry the
   plate home, I have occasion of an houres absence.
BURNISH. With easie consent, sir hast and be carefull.   15

                                    Exit BURNISH.

III. II. S.D. *Burnish*] *Garnish* Q (and throughout this scene); *Burnish is given in
Dramatis Personae.*

MULLIGRUB.   Be very carefull I pray thee to my wifes owne hands.

LIONELL.   Secure your selfe sir.

MULLIGRUB.   To her owne hand.

LIONELL.   Feare not, I have delivered greater thinges than this,   20
to a womans owne hand.

⟨*Exit* LIONELL.⟩

COCLEDEMOY.   Mounsier, please you to buy a fine delicate ball,
sweet ball, a Camphyer ball.

MULLIGRUB.   Pre thee away.

COCLEDEMOY.   Wan' a ball to skower, a skowring ball, a ball   25
to be shaved?

MULLIGRUB.   For the love of god talke not of shaving, I have
been shaved, mischeife and 1000. divells cease him, I have been
shaved.

Exit MULLIGRUB.

COCLEDEMOY.   The Fox growes fat when he is cursed, ile shave   30
ye smother yet. Turd on a tile stone, my lips have a kind of
rhewme at this bole, ile hav't, ile gargalize my throate with this
Vintner, and when I have don with him, spit him out. Ile shark,
conscience does not repine. Were I to bite an honest gentleman
a poore grogaran poet, or a penurious Parson, that had but ten   35
pigs tayles in a twelvemonth and for want of lerning had but one
good stoole in a fortnight, I were damd beyond the workes of
superarrogation, but to wring the whythers of my gowtie barmd
spiggod frigging-jumbler of elements, *Mulligrub*. I hold it as
lawfull as sheepe-shearing, taking egges from hens, caudels from   40
Asses, or butterd shrimps from horses, they make no use of them,
were not provided for them. And therefore worshipfull *Cocledemoy*, hang toasts, on, in grace and vertue to proceed, onely
beware beware degrees, there be rounds in a ladder, and knots in a
halter, ware carts, hang toasts, the comon counsell has decreed it,   45
I must drawe a lot for the great Goblet.

Exit.

25 Wan'] One Q.

⟨SCENE III⟩

Enter MRS MULLIGRUB, *and* LIONELL *with a Goblet.*

MRS MULLIGRUB.   Nay, I pray you stay and drinke, and how
do's your Mistresse, I know her verie well, I have ben inward
with her, and so has many more, she was ever a good patient
creature yfaith, with all my hart ile remember your master an
honest man, he knew me before I was maryed, an honest man hee   5
is, and a crafty, hee comes forward in the world well, I warrant
him, and his wife is a proper woman that she is, well, she has ben
as proper a woman as any in Cheape, she paints now, and yet she
keeps her husbands old Customers to him still. Introth a fine
fac'd wife, in a wainscot carved seat, is a worthy ornament to a   10
Tradesman shop, and an atractive I warrant, her husband shall
finde it in the custome of his ware, Ile assure him, God bee with
you good youth, I acknowledge the receit. *Exit Lionell.* I
acknowledge all the receit sure, tis very well spoken, I acknowledge the receit, thus tis to have good education and to bee   15
brought up in a Taverne. I doe keepe as gallant and as good companie, though I say it, as any she in *London*, Squiers, Gentlemen,
and Knightes diet at my table, and I doe lend some of them money
and full many fine men goe upon my score, as simple as I stand
heere, and I trust them, and truely they verie knightly and   20
courtly promise faire, give me verie good words, and a peece of
flesh when time of yere serves, nay, though my husband be a
Citizen and's caps made of wooll, yet I ha wit, and can see my
good assoone as another, for I have all the thankes. My silly
husband, alasse, hee knowes nothing of it, tis I that beare, tis I 25
that must beare a braine for all.

⟨*Enter* COCLEDEMOY.⟩

COCLEDEMOY.   Faire hower to you Mistresse.
MRS MULLIGRUB.   Faire hower, fine terme, faith ile score it up
anone. A beautiful thought to you sir.
COCLEDEMOY.   Your Husband, and my Maister Mr. *Burnish*   30
has sent you a Jole of fresh Salmon, and they both will come to

III. III. 30 *Burnish*] *Garnish* Q.

dinner to season your new cup with the best wine, which cup
your husband intreats you to send backe by mee, that his armes
may bee grav'd a the side, which he forgot before it was sent.

MRS MULLIGRUB.   By what token, are you sent by no token?   35
Nay, I have wit.

COCLEDEMOY.   He sent me by the same token, that he was dry
shaved this morning.

MRS MULLIGRUB.   A sad token, but true, here sir, I pray you
commend me to your Master, but especially to your Mistresse,   40
tell them they shall be most sincerely welcome.

Exit.

COCLEDEMOY.   Shall be most sincerely welcome, worshipfull
Cocledemoy, lurke close, hang toasts, be not ashamed of thy
qualitie, everie mans turd smels well in's owne nose, vanish
Foyst.   45

Exit.

⟨SCENE IV⟩

Enter MRS MULLIGRUB, *with servants and furniture
for the Table.*

MRS MULLIGRUB.   Come spread these Table Diaper Napkins,
and doe you heare, perfume this Parlour do's so smell of prophane
Tabacco, I could never endure this ungodly Tabacco, since one
of our Elders, assured me upon his knowledge Tabacco was not
used in the Congregation of the family of love. Spread, spread   5
handsomely, Lord these boyes doe things arsie, varsie, you shew
your bringing up, I was a Gentlewoman by my sisters side, I can
tell yee. So methodically: methodically, I wonder where I got
that word. O sir *Aminadab Ruth* bad me kisse him methodically,
I had it somewhere, and I had it indeede.   10

Enter Master MULLIGRUB.

MULLIGRUB.   Mind, be not desperate, ile recover all.
All things with me, shall seeme honest, that can be profitable,
He must nere winch, that would or thrive, or save,
To be cald Nigard, cuckold, Cut-throat, Knave,

III. IV. 8 yee. So] yee so Q.

C

Mrs Mulligrub. Are they come husband?   15

Mulligrub. Who? What, how now? What feast towards in my private Parlour?

Mrs Mulligrub. Pray leave your foolerie, what are they come?

Mulligrub. Come, who come?

Mrs Mulligrub. You need not mak't so strange.   20

Mulligrub. Strange?

Mrs Mulligrub. I strange, you know no man that sent me word, that he and his wife should come to dinner to me, and sent this Jole of fresh Salmon before hand?

Mulligrub. Peace, not I, peace, the Messenger hath mistaken 25 the house, let's eat it up quickly, before it be enquir'd for, sit to it, som vineger, quicke, some good luck yet, faith, I never tasted salmon relisht better, oh when a man feeds at other mens cost.

Mrs Mulligrub. Other mens cost? Why did not you send this Jole of Salmon?   30

Mulligrub. No.

Mrs Mulligrub. By Master *Burnish* man?

Mulligrub. No.

Mrs Mulligrub. Sending me word, that he and his wife would come to dinner to me?   35

Mulligrub. No, no.

Mrs Mulligrub. To season my new bowle?

Mulligrub. Bowle?

Mrs Mulligrub. And withall wild me to send the bowle backe?

Mulligrub. Backe?   40

Mrs Mulligrub. That you might have your Armes grav'd on the side?

Mulligrub. Ha?

Mrs Mulligrub. By the same token you were drie shaven this morning before you went forth.   45

Mulligrub. Pah, how this Sammon stinkes.

Mrs Mulligrub. And thereupon sent the bowle backe, prepar'd dinner, nay and I bare not a braine.

Mulligrub. Wife, doe not vexe me, is the bowle gone, is it deliver'd?   50

Mrs Mulligrub. Delivered! Yes sure, tis delivered.

32 *Burnish*] Garnish Q.

MULLIGRUB. I will never more say my prayers, doe not make
mee madde, tis common, let me not crie like a woman, is it gone?
MRS MULLIGRUB.   Gone? Good is my witnesse, I delivered it
with no more intention to be cozend on't, than the child new   55
borne: and yet
MULLIGRUB.   Looke to my house, I am haunted with evill
spirites, here mee, doe; heare me, if I have not my Goblet againe,
heaven, I'le to the Divell, I'le to a Conjurer, looke to my house,
I'le raise all the wise men ithe streete.   60
⟨*Exit* MULLIGRUB.⟩

MRS MULLIGRUB.   Deliver us! What wordes are these, I trust in
God, hee is but drunke sure.

Enter COCLEDEMOY.

COCLEDEMOY ⟨*aside*⟩.   I must have the Sammon to. Worshipfull *Cocledemoy*, now for the Master peece, God blesse thy necke
peece, and *Fowtra*. ⟨*To* MRS MULLIGRUB⟩ Faire Mistresse my   65
Master.
MRS MULLIGRUB.   Have I caught you, what *Roger*!
COCLEDEMOY.   Peace good Mistres, I'le tell you all, a Jest, a
verie mere Jest, your husband onely tooke sport to fright you,
the bowl's at my Masters, and there is your husband, who sent   70
me in all hast, least you should be over frighted with his
fayning, to come to dinner to him.
MRS MULLIGRUB.   Praise Heaven, it is no worse.
COCLEDEMOY.   And desired me, to desire you to send the Jole
of Sammon before, and your selfe to come after to them, my   75
Mistresse would bee right glad to see you.
MRS MULLIGRUB.   I pray carry it: now thanke them entierly:
blesse me, I was never so out of my skinne in my life, pray thanke
your Mistresse most entirely.
COCLEDEMOY ⟨*aside*⟩.   So now *Figo*. Worshipfull *Mall Faugh*, 80
and I will monch. Cheaters and Bawds go together like washing
and wringing.
                                                            Exit.

63–4 to. Worshipfull] to worship; Qᵘ; to, worship: Qᶜ.
80 *Figo*. Worshipfull] Figo‸ worshipfull Q.

MRS MULLIGRUB.   Beshrew his heart for his labor, how every thing about me quivers. What *Christian*! My hat and aporne; ⟨*Enter* CHRISTIAN⟩ here take my sleeves, and how I tremble,   85 so ile gossope it now for't, thats certaine, here has been revolutions, and false fiers indeed.

⟨*Exit* CHRISTIAN.⟩

Enter MULLIGRUB.

MULLIGRUB.   Whether now? Whats the matter with you now? Whether are you a gadding?

MRS MULLIGRUB.   Come, come, play the foole no more: Will   90 you goe?

MULLIGRUB.   Whether, in the ranke name of madnesse: whether?

MRS MULLIGRUB.   Whether? Why to mayster *Burnish* to eate the Jowle of Salmon? Lord, how strange you make it!   95

MULLIGRUB.   Why so, why so?

MRS MULLIGRUB.   Why so? Why did not you send the selfe-same fellow for the Jole of Salmon, that had the cup?

MULLIGRUB.   Tis well, tis very well.

MRS MULLIGRUB.   And wild me to come and eate it with you   100 at the Goldsmithes?

MULLIGRUB.   O I, I, I, art in thy right wits?

MRS MULLIGRUB.   Doe you heare, make a foole of some body else, and you make an asse of me. Ile make an Oxe of you, do ye see?   105

MULLIGRUB.   Nay wife be patient, for looke you, I may be madde, or drunke, or so, for my owne part, though you can bear more then I, yet I can do well: I will not cursse nor cry, but heaven knows what I thinke. Come, lets goe heare some musicke, I will never more say my praiers. Lets goe heare some   110 dolefull musicke. Nay if Heaven forget to prosper knaves Ile goe no more to the Synagogue. Now I am discontented, Ile turne Sectarie that is fashion.

Exeunt.

84 me quivers. What *Christian!* My] me quiuers, what *Christian* my Q.
94 *Burnish*] Garnish Q.
108 cry] BULLEN; cary Q.

ACT IV

SCENE I

Enter SIR HUBERT SUBBOYS, SIR LIONELL FREEVILL,
CRISPINELLA, *servants with lightes.*

SIR HUBERT.   More lights: welcome *Sir Lionell Freevill,* brother
Freevill shortly. Looke to your lights.
SERVANT.   The Maskers are at hand.
⟨SIR HUBERT.⟩   Call downe our daughter: Harke they are at
hande, ranke handsomly.   5

Enter the Masquers, they daunce. Enter MALHEUREUX *and take*
BEATRICE *from* FREEVILL. *They draw.*

FREEVILL.   Know sir, I have the advantage of the place,
You are not safe, I would deale even with you.

                                   They exchange gloves as pledges.
MALHEUREUX.   So.
FREEVILL.   So.
BEATRICE.   I doe beseech you sweet, do not for me provoke your   10
Fortune.
SIR LIONELL.   What sodaine flaw is risen?
SIR HUBERT.   From whence coms this?
FREEVILL.   An ulcer long time lurking, now is burst.
SIR HUBERT.   Good sir the time and your deseigns are soft.   15
BEATRICE.   I deare sir, councell him, advise him, twill rellish well
From your carving: Good my sweet rest safe.
FREEVILL.   Als well, als well, this shall be ended straight.
SIR HUBERT.   The banquet staies, there weele discourse more
large.   20
FREEVILL.   Marriage must not make men Cowards.
SIR LIONELL.   Nor rage fooles.

IV. I. 4 SIR HUBERT] BRERETON; *Sir Lyo.* Q.

SIR HUBERT. "Tis valor not where heat, but reason rules.

Exeunt all but TYSEFEW *and* CRISPINELLA.

TYSEFEW. But do you heare Lady, you proud ape you,
What was the Jest you brake of me even now?   25

CRISPINELLA. Nothing, I onely saide you were all mettle, that
you had a brazen face, a Leaden braine, and a copper beard.

TYSEFEW. Quicksilver, thou little more then a Dwarfe, and
something lesse then a Woman.

CRISPINELLA. A Wispe, a wispe, a wispe, will you go to the   30
banquet?

TYSEFEW. By the Lord I thinke thou wilt marry shortly too,
thou growest somewhat foolish already.

CRISPINELLA. O Ifaith, tis a faire thing to be married, and a
necessary. To hear this word, *must.* If our husbands be proud,   35
we must bear his contempt, if noysome we must beare with the
Gote under his armcholes, if a foole we must beare his bable,
and which is worse, if a loose liver, wee must live uppon un-
holsome Reversions: Where, on the contrary side, our husbands
because they may, and we must; care not for us. Thinges hop'd   40
with feare, and got with struglings, are mens high pleasures,
when duety pales and flattes their appetite.

TYSEFEW. What a tart Monkey is this, by heaven if thou hadst
not so much wit I could finde in my hart to marry thee. Faith
bear with me for all this.   45

CRISPINELLA. Beare with thee, I wonder how thy mother
could beare thee ten months in her bellie, when I cannot indure
thee 2. hours in mine eie.

TYSEFEW. Alasse for you sweet soule, by the Lorde you are
growne a proud, scurvie, apish, ydle, disdainefull, scoffing, Gods 50
foot, because you have read *Euphues and his England,* Palmerin
de Oliva, and the Legend of Lies.

CRISPINELLA. Why yfaith yet servant, you of all others
shoulde beare with my knowne unmalicious humors, I have

---

23 S.D. *Exeunt all but* TYSEFEW *and* CRISPINELLA] *Exit.* | *Onely Tissefu and*
*Crispin*ₐ *stay.* Qᵘ; *Exit.* | *Onely Tissefu and Crispin. stay*ₐ Qᶜ.
35 word, *must.* If] word must, if Qᵘ; word, *must,* if Qᶜ.
44 to marry] to my marry Q.
51 *Euphues*] *Ephius* Qᵘ; *Ephues* Qᶜ.

alwaies in my hart given you your due respect: And heaven   55
may be sworne, I have privately given faire speach of you, and
protested.

TYSEFEW.   Nay looke you, for my owne part, if I have not as
religiously vowd my hart to you, been drunke to your health,
swalowd flap-dragons, eate glasses, drunke urine, stabd armes,   60
and don all the offices of protested gallantrie for your sake: and
yet you tell me I have a brazen face, a leaden braine: and a copper
bearde, Come yet and it please you.

CRISPINELLA.   No, no, you do not love me?

TYSEFEW.   By ( ) but I do now, and whosoever dares say that   65
I do not love you, nay honor you, and if you would vouchsafe
to marrie.

CRISPINELLA.   Naie as for that thinke ont as you will, but
Gods my record, and my sister knowes I have taken drinke and
slept uppont, that if ever I marrie it shall be you, and I will   70
marrie, and yet I hope I do not saie it shall be you neither.

TYSEFEW.   By heaven I shalbe assoone wearie of health as of
your injoyeng: will you cast a smooth cheeke upon me?

CRISPINELLA.   I cannot tell, I have no crumpt shoulders, my
back needs no mantle, and yet marriage is honorable: do you   75
thinke ye shall prove a Cuckold?

TYSEFEW.   No, by the Lord, not I!

CRISPINELLA.   Why, I thanke you yfaith:
Heigho: I slept on my backe this morning
And dreamt the strangest dreames: 80
Good Lord, how things will come to passe?
Will you go to the banquet?

TYSEFEW.   If you will bee mine, you shall be your owne, my
pursse, my bodie, my hart is yours, onlie bee silent in my house,
modest at my table, and wanton in my bed, and the Empresse of   85
Europe cannot content, and shall not be contented better.

CRISPINELLA.   Can anie kind hart speake more discreetlie
affectionatelie: my fathers consent, and as for mine,

TYSEFEW.   Then thus, and thus ⟨*Kissing her*⟩, so Hymen should
begin,

Sometimes a falling out, proves falling in.   90

Exeunt.

⟨SCENE II⟩

Enter FREEVILL, *speaking to some within,*
MALHEUREUX *at the other dore.*

FREEVILL.   As you respect my vertue, give me leave
To satisfie my reason, though not bloud.
So, all runs right, our fained rage hath tane
To fullest life, they are much possest
Of force most, most all quarrell: now my right friend   5
Resolve me with open brest, free and true hart
Cannot thy vertue having space to thinke
And fortifie her weakened powers with reason,
Discourses, Meditations, Discipline,
Divine ejaculatories, and all those aydes against devils: 10
Cannot all these curbe thy lowe appetite
And sensuall furie?
MALHEUREUX.   "There is no God in bloud, no reason in desire:
Shall I but live? Shall I not be forc't to act
Some deed, whose verie name is hydeous?   15
FREEVILL.   No.
MALHEUREUX.   Then I must enjoy *Francischina.*
FREEVILL.   You shall: Ile lend this ring, shew it to that faire
Devill, it will resolve me dead, which rumor with my artificiall
absence, wil make most firme. Enjoy her sodainlie.   20
MALHEUREUX.   But if report go strong that you are slaine, and
that by me? Whereon I may be seizd. Where shall I find your
being?
FREEVILL.   At maister Shatewes the Jewellers, to whose breast
Ile trust our secret purpose.   25
MALHEUREUX.   I rest your selfe, each man hath follies.
FREEVILL.   But those worst of all,
"Who with a willing eie, do seeing fall.
MALHEUREUX.   Tis true, but truth seemes folly in madnesse
                                        spectacles,
I am not now my selfe, no man: Farewell.   30
FREEVILL.   Farewell.

MALHEUREUX. "When woman's in the hart, in the soule hell.

Exit MALHEUREUX.

FREEVILL.   Now repentance the fooles whip seize thee,
Nay if there be no meanes Ile be thy friend.
But not thy Vices; and with greatest sence   35
Ile force thee feele thy errors, to the worst
The vildest of dangers thou shalt sinke into.
No Jeweller shall see me, I will lurke
Where none shall know or thinke, close Ile withdraw,
And leave thee with two friendes: a whore and knave.   40
But is this vertue in me? No, not pure,
Nothing extreamely best with us endures,
No use in simple purities, the elementes
Are mixt for use, Silver without alay
Is all to eager to be wrought for use: 45
Nor precise vertues ever purely good
Holdes usefull size with temper of weake bloud:
Then let my course be borne, tho: with side-wind,
The end being good, the meanes are well assignd.

Exit

⟨SCENE III⟩

Enter FRANCISCHINA *melancholy*,
COCLEDEMOY *leading her.*

COCLEDEMOY.   Come catafugo Francke a Franck-hall, *who who*
ho,
Excellent, Ha, heers a plump rumpt wench, with a breast
Softer then a Courtyers tongue, an old Ladies gums,
Or an old mans *mentula*, my fine Rogue.
FRANCISCHINA.   Pah you poultron.   5
COCLEDEMOY.   Gooddy fiste, flumpum pumpum, a my fine
Wagtaile,
Thou art as false as prostituted and adulcerate as some translated
manuscript. Busse fayre whore, busse.
FRANCISCHINA.   Gods sacrament, Pox.

COCLEDEMOY.   *Hadamoy key dost thou frowne medianthon teukey*   10
Nay look heer: *Numeron key* Silver *blithefor cany*
Os cany goblet: *Us key ne moy blegefoy oteeston pox*
On you Gosling.
FRANCISCHINA.   By me fait dis bin verie fine langage, Ick sall
bush ye now, ha, be garzon vare had you dat plate?   15
COCLEDEMOY.   *Hedemoy key*, get you gon Punck rampant, *key*
common up-taile.

Enter MARY FAUGH, *in hast.*

MARY FAUGH.   O daughter, cozen, neece, servant, mistresse.
COCLEDEMOY.   Humpum, plumpum squat, I am gone.

Exit COCLEDEMOY.

MARY FAUGH.   There is one M. *Malheureux* at the dore desires   20
to see you: he saies he must not be denide, for he hath sent you
this ring and withall saies tis done.
FRANCISCHINA.   Vat sall me do now, Gods sacramant: tell him
two howers hence he sall be most affectionatlie velcome, tell him
(vat sal me do) tel him Ick am bin in my bate, and Ick sall   25
perfume my seetes, mak a mine bodie so delicate for his arme.
Two houres hence.
MARY FAUGH.   I shall satisfie him. Two houres hence. Well.

Exit MARY FAUGH.

FRANCISCHINA.   Now Ick sall revange, hay, begar me sal tartar
de whole generation, mine braine vorke it,   30
Freevill, is dead, *Malheureux* sall hang,
And mine rivall *Beatrice*, Ick sall make run madde.

Enter MARY FAUGH.

MARY FAUGH.   Hees gone forsooth to eate a cawdle of Cock-
stones, and will returne within this two houres.
FRANCISCHINA.   Verie vel, give monis to some fellow to squire   35
me, Ick sal go abroad.

IV. III. 17 common up-taile] common vp-taile Qᶜ; *comen vp-tale* Qᵘ.
28 him. Two] him two Q.
28 hence. Well] hence well Q.

MARY FAUGH.   Thers a lustie *Bravo* beneath, a stranger, but a
    good stale Rascall: he sweares valiantlie, kicks a Bawd right
    vertuously, and protestes with an emptie pocket right desperately,
    Heele squier you.   40
FRANCISCHINA.   Very velcom, mine fan, Ick sall retorne
    presantly. ⟨*Exit* MARY FAUGH.⟩ Now sal me be revange ten
    tousant devla, der sall be no got in me but passion, no tought
    but rage, no mercie but bloud, no spirit but Diula in me,
    Dere sal noting tought good for me,   45
    But dat is mischievous for others.

                                                              Exit.

                          ⟨SCENE IV⟩

                 Enter SIR HUBERT, SIR LIONELL, BEATRICE,
              CRISPINELLA, *and* NURSE. TYSEFEW *following.*

SIR LIONELL.   Did no one see him since? Pray God, nay all is
                                                              well,
    A litle heat, what he is but withdrawne? And yet I would to God,
    But feare you nothing.
BEATRICE.   Pray God that all be well or would I were not.
TYSEFEW.   Hees not to be found Sir any where.   5
SIR LIONELL.   You must not make a heavy face presage an ill
    event: I like your Sister well, shees quick and lively: would she
    woulde marry faith.
CRISPINELLA.   Marry, nay and I would marry: methinks an old
    mans a quiet thing.   10
SIR LIONELL.   Ha, masse and so he is.
CRISPINELLA.   You are a Widdower.
SIR LIONELL.   That I am Ifaith faire *Crispinella* and I can tell
    you, would you affect me, I have it in me yet Ifaith.
CRISPINELLA.   Troth I am in love, let me see your hand: would   15
    you cast your selfe away upon me willingly?
SIR LIONELL.   Will I: I by the ( )
CRISPINELLA.   Woulde you be a Cockould willingly? By my
    troath tis a comely, fine, and handsome sight, for one of my
    yeeres to marry an old man, truth tis restorative, what a comfort-   20
    able thinge it is to thinke of her husband, to heare his venerable

cough a the everlastings, to feele his rough skinne, his summer
handes, and winter legges, his almoste no eies, and assuredly no
teeth, and then to thinke what she must dreame of, when she
considers others happines and her owne want: tis a worthy and   25
notorious comfortable match.

SIR LIONELL.   Pish, pish, will you have me?

CRISPINELLA.   Will you assure me?

SIR LIONELL.   Five hundred pound joynture.

CRISPINELLA.   That you will die within this fortnight?   30

SIR LIONELL.   No, by my faith *Crispinella*.

CRISPINELLA.   Then *Crispinella* by her faith assures you sheele
have none of you.

Enter FREEVILL *disguised like a pandor and* FRANCISCHINA.

FREEVILL.   Beere leave Gentles and men of nightcaps, I would
speak, but that here stands one is able to expresse her owne tale   35
best.

FRANCISCHINA.   Sir mine speech is to you, you had a sonne
matre *Freevill*.

SIR LIONELL.   Had ha, and have.

FRANCISCHINA.   No point, me am come to assure you dat on   40
mestre *Malheureux* hath killed him.

BEATRICE.   O me, wretched, wretched.

SIR HUBERT.   Looke to our daughter.

SIR LIONELL.   How art thou informed?

FRANCISCHINA.   If dat it please you to go vid me, Ick sall bring   45
you where you sall hear *Malheureux* vid his owne lips confesse
it, and dare ye may apprehend him, and revenge your and mine
loves bloud.

SIR HUBERT.   Your loves bloud mistresse, was he your Love?

FRANCISCHINA.   He was so sir, let your daughter heare it: do   50
not veep Lady, de yong man dat be slaine did not love you, for
hee still lovitt me ten tousant tousant times more deerely.

BEATRICE.   O my hart I will love you the better, I cannot hate
what he affected! O passion, O my griefe which way will break,
thinke and consume?   55

CRISPINELLA.   Peace.

BEATRICE.   Deare woes cannot speake.

FRANCISCHINA.   For looke you Ladie dis your ring he gave me,
   vid most bitter jests at your scornd kindnesse.

BEATRICE.   He did not ill not to love me, but sure hee did not   60
   well to mocke me: Gentle mindes will pittie, though they cannot
   love: yet peace, and my love sleepe with him. Unlace good
   nurce, alas, I was not so ambitious of so supreme an happinesse,
   that he should onlie love me, twas joy enough for me poore soule
   that I only might onlie love him.   65

FRANCISCHINA.   O but to be abusde, scornde, scoft at, O ten
   tousand divla by such a one, and unto such a one.

BEATRICE.   I thinke you saie not true sister, shall we know one
   another in the other world?

CRISPINELLA.   What meanes my sister?   70

BEATRICE.   I would faine see him againe: O my torturd mind,
   Freevill is more then dead, he is unkinde.

   Exit BEATRICE *and* CRISPINELLA *and* NURSE.

SIR HUBERT.   Convey her in, and so sir as you said set a strong
   watch.

SIR LIONELL.   I sir, and so passe along with this same common   75
   woman, you must make it good.

FRANCISCHINA.   Ick sall, or let me pay for his, mine bloud.

SIR HUBERT.   Come then along all, with quiet speed.

SIR LIONELL.   O Fate?

TYSEFEW.   O sir, be wisely sorrie, but not passionate.   80

                                   Exeunt.
                         Manet FREEVILL.

FREEVILL.   I will goe and reveale my selfe: staie: no, no,
   Greefe endeeres Love: Heaven to have such a wife
   Is happinesse, to breed pale envy in the saintes.
   Thou worthy Dove-like virgin without gall,
   Cannot (that womans evill) Jealousie,   85
   Despight disgrace, nay which is worst, contempt
   Once stirre thy faith. O Truth, how few sisters hast thou?
   Deere memorie, with what a suffring sweetnesse, quiet modesty,
   Yet deepe affection she receiv'd my death,
   And then with what a patient, yet oppressed kindnesse   90

She tooke my leudlie intimated wrongs. O the derest of heaven!
Were there but three such women in the world, two
Might be saved.
Well, I am great with expectation to what devilish end
This woman of foule soul will drive her plots: 95
But providence all wicked art ore-tops.
"And Impudence must know (tho stiffe as Ice,)
"That fortune doth not alway dote on Vice.

                                                 Exit.

⟨SCENE V⟩

Enter SIR HUBERT, SIR LIONELL, TYSEFEW,
FRANCISCHINA *and three with Halberds.*

SIR HUBERT.   Plant a watch there, be verie carefull Sirs, the rest
with us.
TYSEFEW.   The heavy night growes to her depth of quiet, tis
about mid darkenesse.
FRANCISCHINA.   Mine shambre is hard by, Ick sall bring you to   5
it presantment.
SIR LIONELL.   Deepe silence. On.

                                               Exeunt.

⟨SCENE VI⟩

COCLEDEMOY [*Within*]. *Wa, ha, ho.*

Enter MULLIGRUB.

MULLIGRUB.   It was his voice, tis he: he suppes with his cupping glasses. Tis late, he must passe this waie: Ile ha him, Ile ha
my fine boy, my worshipfull *Cocledemoy*, Ile moy him, he shall
be hangd in lowsie linnen, Ile hire some sectary to make him   5

IV. IV. 91 heaven!] heauen? Q.
IV. V. 7 On. *Exeunt.*] On*Cocle. within Wa, ha, ho,   Ex.* Q^u; On *Cocle. within
Wa, ha, ho,   Ex.* Q^c.
IV. VI. 1 [*Within*] *Wa, ha, ho.*] from IV. V. 7, *see above.*

an hereticke before he die! And when he is dead Ile pisse on his grave.

Enter COCLEDEMOY.

COCLEDEMOY.   Ah my fine puncks, good night, Franke Frailtie, Fraile a Fraile-Hall! *Bonus noches my ubiquitari.*
MULLIGRUB.   Ware polling and shaving Sir.   10
COCLEDEMOY.   A Wolfe, a wolfe, a wolfe.

> *Exit* COCLEDEMOY, *leaving his cloke behind him.*

MULLIGRUB.   Heers something yet, a Cloke, a cloke, yet Ile after, he cannot scape the watch, Ile hang him if I have any mercy, Ile slice him.

> *Exit.*

⟨SCENE VII⟩

Enter COCLEDEMOY ⟨*and* THE WATCH, *separately*⟩.

FIRST CONSTABLE.   Who goes there? Come before the Constable.
COCLEDEMOY.   Bread a God Constable, you are a Watch for the devil. Honest men are robd under your nose. Thers a false knave in the habit of a Vintner, set upon me, he would have had my   5 purse, but I tooke me to my heeles: yet he got my Cloke, a plaine stuffe cloke poore, yet twill serve to hang him? Tis my losse, poor man that I am.

> ⟨*Exit* COCLEDEMOY.⟩

SECOND CONSTABLE.   Maisters, we must Watch better, ist not strange that knaves, Drunkerds, and theeves, should be a brode,   10 and yet we of the Watch, Scriveners, Smithes, and Taylors, never stur.

Enter MULLIGRUB *running with* COCLEDEMOYS *cloke.*

⟨FIRST CONSTABLE.⟩   Harke, who goes there?
MULLIGRUB.   An honest man and a Cittiezen.

        8–9 Franke Frailtie, Fraile] Franke, frailtie, fraile W.
        10 MULLIGRUB.] *Mal.* Q^u; *Mul.* Q^c.
        IV. VII. 12 SD. *Follows line* 8 *in* Q.
        13 FIRST CONSTABLE] 2. Q; CONSTABLE 1 1633.

SECOND CONSTABLE.   Appeare, appeare what are you?   15
MULLIGRUB.   A simple Vintner.
FIRST CONSTABLE.   A Vintner ha, and simple, draw neerer, nerer: heers the Cloke.
SECOND CONSTABLE.   I Maister Vintner we know you, a plaine stuffe cloke: tis it.   20
FIRST CONSTABLE.   Right, come: Oh thou varlet, doest not thou know that the wicked cannot scape the eies of the Constable?
MULLIGRUB.   What meanes this violence? As I am an honest man I tooke the cloke.   25
FIRST CONSTABLE.   As you are a knave, you tooke the cloke, we are your witnesses for that.
MULLIGRUB.   But heare me, heare me, Ile tell you what I am.
SECOND CONSTABLE.   A theefe you are.
MULLIGRUB.   I tell you my name is *Mulligrub*.   30
FIRST CONSTABLE.   I will grubbe you! In with him to the stockes, there let him sit tell to morrow morning that Justice Quodlibet may examine him.
MULLIGRUB.   Why but I tell thee.
SECOND CONSTABLE.   Why but I tel thee, weele tell thee now.   35
MULLIGRUB.   Am I not mad, am I not an asse?
Why scabs, Gods-foot: let me out.
SECOND CONSTABLE.   I, I, let him prate, he shall find matter in us scabs I warrant: Gods-so, what good members of the common wealth doo wee prove.   40
FIRST CONSTABLE.   Prethee peace, lets remember our duties, and let go sleepe, in the feare of God.
                                            Exeunt.
                        Having left MULLIGRUB *in the stocks.*
MULLIGRUB.   Who goes there? Illo, ho, ho! Zounds shall I run mad,
Loose my wits: shall I be hangd? Hark: who goes there? Do not   45
feare to be poore *Mulligrub*,
Thou hast a sure stocke now.
Enter COCLEDEMOY *like a Belman.*
COCLEDEMOY.   The night growes old,
                    And many a cockould

Is now—*Wha, ha, ha, ho,*   50
Maids on their backes,
Dreame of sweet smackes,
And warme: *Wo, ho, ho, ho.*
I must go comfort my venerable *Mullibrub*, I must fiddle him till
he fyst: fough: 55
Maides in your Night-railes,
Looke well to your light (-)
Keepe close your lockes,
And downe your smocks,
Keepe a brode eie   60
And a close thigh.
Excellent, excellent, whose there? Now Lord, Lord, (maister
Mulligrub) deliver us: what does your Worship in the stocks?
I pray come our Sir.

MULLIGRUB.   Zounds man I tell thee I am lockt.   65

COCLEDEMOY.   Lockt: O world: O men: O time: o night: that
canst not discerne vertue, and wisdome, and one of the common
Counsel:
What is your Worship in for?

MULLIGRUB.   For (a plague ont) suspition of Fellonie.   70

COCLEDEMOY.   Nay, and it be but such a trifle, Lord I could
weep, to see your good Worship in this taking: your Worshippe
has beene a good friend to me, and tho you have forgot me, yet
I knewe your wife before she was married, and since I have
found your Worships dore open and I have knockt, and God   75
knows what I have saved: and doe I live to see your Worship
stockt?

MULLIGRUB.   Honest Belman, I perceive thou knowest me, I
prethe call the Watch.
Informe the Constable of my reputation,   80
That I may no longer abide in this shamefull habitation,
And hold thee, all I have about me.

Gives him his pursse.

COCLEDEMOY.   Tis more then I deserve sir: Let me alone for
your Deliverie.

49 and 50 *One line in* Q.   52 and 53 *One line in* Q.
61 and 62 *One line in* Q.   75 Worships] Worsh. Q.

MULLIGRUB.   Doe, and then let me alone with *Cocledemoy*,   85
Ile moy him.

⟨*Enter* THE WATCH.⟩

COCLEDEMOY.   Maids in your—
Maister Constable, whose that ith'stoks?
FIRST CONSTABLE.   One for a robberie: one *Mulligrub*, he cals
himselfe.   90
⟨COCLEDEMOY.⟩   *Mulligrub?*
FIRST CONSTABLE.   Bel-man, knowst thou him?
COCLEDEMOY.   Know him! O maister Constable what good
service have you done. Know him? Hees a strong theefe, his
house has beene suspected for a bawdie Taverne a great while: 95
and a receipt for Cut-purses, tis most certaine: He has beene
long in the blacke booke, and is he tane now?
SECOND CONSTABLE.   Berlady my maisters weele not trust the
stocks with him, weele have him to the Justices, get a *Mittimus*
to Newgate presentlie. Come sir, come on sir.   100
MULLIGRUB.   Ha: does your Rascalship yet know my Worship
In the end?
FIRST CONSTABLE.   I, the end of your Worship we know.
MULLIGRUB.   Ha, goodman Constable, heeres an honest fellow
can tell you what I am!   105
SECOND CONSTABLE.   Tis true sir, yare a strong theefe hee
saies on his owne knowledge: Binde fast, binde fast, we know
you: Weele trust no Stocks with you. Awaie with him to the
Jayle instantlie.
MULLIGRUB.   Why but dost heare Bel-man, Rogue, Rascall,   110
Gods Whie but?

The CONSTABLE *drags awaie* MULLIGRUB.

COCLEDEMOY.   Whie but; *wha, ha, ha;* excellent, excellent, ha
my fine *Cocledemoy*, my Vintner fistes, Ile make him fart crackers
before I ha done with him; to morrow is the daie of Judgment.
Afore the Lord God my knaverie growes unperegall,   115

87 and 88 *One line in* Q.
91 COCLEDEMOY] *editorial addition.*
91 and 92 *Run on in* Q *continuing First Constable's from* 90.
96 and] Q^c: But Q^u.

Tis time to take a nap, untill halfe an houre hence:
God give your Worships Musicke, content, and rest.

Exeunt.

ACT V

SCENE I

Enter FRANCISCHINA, SIR LIONELL, TYSEFEW,
with Officers ⟨*and* FREEVILL, *disguised*⟩.

FRANCISCHINA. You bin verie velcom to mine shambra.
SIR LIONELL. But how knowe ye, how are ye assurde
  Both of the deed, and of his sure returne.
FRANCISCHINA. O Myn-here. Ick sall tell you; metre *Malheu-*
                                                    reux
  Came all bretlesse running a my shambra   5
  His sword all bloudie: he tel a me he had kil *Freevill*,
  And pred a me to conceale him:
  Ick flatter him, bid bring monies, he should live and lie vid me,
  He went whilst Ick (me hope vidout sins) out of mine
  Mush love to *Freevill* betraie him.   10
SIR LIONELL. Feare not, tis well: good works get grace for sin.

                She conceales them behinde the curtaine.

FRANCISCHINA. Dere, peace, rest dere, so softlie, all goe in.
  De net is laie, now sal Ick be revenge.
  If dat me knew a dog dat *Freevill* love,
  Me would puisson him, for know de deepest hell   15
  As a revenging Womans, naught so fell.

Enter MARY FAUGH.

MARY FAUGH. Ho Cosen Francke, the partie you wot of,
  M. *Malheureux.*
FRANCISCHINA. Bid him come up, I prede.
                Cantat saltatque cum cithera.
Enter MALHEUREUX.

117 Worships] Worship Q.   v. 1. 4 Myn-here] Qᶜ; Man-here Qᵘ.

FRANCISCHINA.   O min here man, a dere liver Love,   20
   Mine ten tousant times velcom Love,
   Ha, by mine trat, you bin de just, vat sall me saie:
   Vat seet honie name sall I call you?
MALHEUREUX.   Anie from you is pleasure. Come my loving
   Prettinesse, wheres thie Chamber?   25
   I long to touch your sheetes.
FRANCISCHINA.   No, no, not yet mine seetest soft-lipped love:
   You sall not gulp downe all delights at once:
   Be min trat, dis all-fles-Lovers, dis ravenous Wenches
   Dat sallow all downe hole, vill have all at one bit,   30
   Fie, fie, fie, be min fait dey do eate
   Comfets vid spoones.
   No, no, Ile make you chew your pleasure vit love,
   "De more degrees and steps, de more delight,
   "De more endeered is de pleasure hight.   35
MALHEUREUX.   What, your a lerned wanton, and proceed by art?
FRANCISCHINA.   Go little vag, pleasure should have a
   Cranes long necke, to relish de Ambrosia of Delight.
   And Ick pre de tel me, for me loves to heare of manhood
   Verie mush, Ifait: Ick prede (vat vas me a saieng)   40
   Oh, Ick prede tell a me:
   How did you killa metre *Freevill*?
MALHEUREUX.   Why quareld a set purpose, drew him out,
   Singled him, and having th'advantage of my sword
   And might, ran him through and through.   45
FRANCISCHINA.   Vat did you vid him van he was sticken?
MALHEUREUX.   I dragd him by the heeles to the next wharffe
   and spurnd him in the River.

                Those in ambush rusheth forth and take him.

SIR LIONELL.   Seize, seize him: O monsterous! O ruthlesse
   Villaine!   50
MALHEUREUX.   What meane you Gentlemen? By heaven,
TYSEFEW.   Speake not of anie thing thats good.
MALHEUREUX.   Your error gives you passion: *Freevill* lives.
SIR LIONELL.   Thie own lips saie, thou liest.

                48 S.D. *take*] 1633; *takes* Q.

MALHEUREUX. Let me die if at Shatewes the Jeweller, he lives   55
  not safe untoucht.
TYSEFEW. Meane time to stricktest guard, to sharpest prison.
MALHEUREUX. No rudenesse Gentlemen: Ile go undragd. O
  wicked, wicked Divell.

                                                              Exit.

SIR LIONELL. Sir, the daie of triall is this morn,   60
  Lets prosecute the sharpest rigor, and severest end:
  "Good men are cruell, when the'are vices friend.
SIR HUBERT. Woman we thanke thee, with no emptie hand,
  Strumpets are fit, fit for som-thing. Farewell.

                               All save FREEVILL *depart.*

FREEVILL. I, for Hell: O thou unrepriveable, beyond all   65
  Measure of Grace dambd immediatlie:
  That things of beautie created for sweet use:
  Soft comfort, and as the verie musicke of life,
  Custome should make so unutterablie hellish!
  O heaven: what difference is in women, and their life?   70
  What man, but worthie name of Man,
  Would leave the modest pleasures of a lawfull bed,
  The holie union of two equall harts
  Mutuallie holding either deere as health,
  The undoubted yssues, Joyes of chast sheetes,   75
  The unfained imbrace of sober Ignorance:
  To twine the unhealthfull loynes of common Loves,
  The prostituted impudence of things.
  Sencelesse like those by *Cataracks* of Nyle,
  "Their use so vile, takes awaie sence, how vile   80
  "To love a creature, made of bloud and hell,
  "Whose use makes weake, whose companie doth shame,
  "Whose bed doth begger: yssue doth defame.

Enter FRANCISCHINA.

FRANCISCHINA. Metre *Freevill* live: ha, ha, live at mestre
                                                    Shatewes:

  64 S.D. *depart*] *departs* Q.   66 dambd] Q^c; doombd Q^u.
            77 twine] Q^c; twaine Q^u.

Mush at metre Shatews. *Freevill* is dead. *Malheureux* sall hang,   85
And swete divel, dat *Beatrice* would but run mad, dat
She would but run mad, den me would dance and sing.
Metre *Don Dubon*, me pre ye now go to Mestres
Beatrice, tel her *Freevill* is sure ded, and dat he
Cursse hir selfe especiallie, for dat he was   90
Sticked in hir quarrell, swering in his last gaspe,
Dat if it had bin in mine quarrels,
Twould never have greeved him.

FREEVILL.   I will.

FRANCISCHINA.   Prede do, and saie anie ting dat vil vex her.   95

FREEVILL.   Let me alone to vex her.

FRANCISCHINA.   Vil you, vil you mak a her run mad? Here take
Dis ring, sea me scorne to wear anie ting dat was hers,
Or his: I prede torment her. Ick cannot love her,
She honest and vertuous forsooth.   100

FREEVILL.   Is she so? O vile creature! Then let me alone with
her.

FRANCISCHINA.   Vat. Vil you mak a her mad? Seet by min trat,
Be pretta servan, Bush, Ick sall go to bet now.

⟨*Exit* FRANCISCHINA.⟩

FREEVILL.   Mischiefe whether wilt thou? O thou tear-lesse
woman!
How monstrous is thy Devill,   105
The end of Hell as thee.
How miserable were it to be vertuous, if thou couldst prosper?
Ile to my Love, the faithfull *Beatrice*,
She has wept enough, and faith deere soule too much.
But yet how sweet it is to thinke   110
How deere ones life was to his Love: how moornd his death.
Tis Joy not to be exprest with breath:
But O let him that would such passion drinke,
Be quiet of his speech, and onlie thinke.
Exit.

102 Vat] Q^c; I dat Q^u.

⟨SCENE II⟩

Enter BEATRICE *and* CRISPINELLA.

BEATRICE.   Sister, cannot a woman kill her selfe? Is it not lawful
to die when we should not live?

CRISPINELLA.   O sister tis a question not for us, we must do
what God will.

BEATRICE.   What God will? Alasse, can torment be his glorie,   5
or our greefe his pleasure? Does not the Nurces nipple juic'd
over with Wormwood, bid the childe it should not sucke? And
does not Heaven when it hath made our breath bitter unto us,
say we shud not live? O my best sister: to suffer wounds when
one may scape this rod, is against nature, that is against God.   10

CRISPINELLA.   Good sister do not make me weep: sure *Freevill*
was not false: Ile gage my life that strumpet out of craft and
some close second end hath malist him.

BEATRICE.   O sister if he were not false, whom have I lost?
If he were: what griefe to such unkindnesse,   15
From head to foote I am all myserie:
Onely in this, some justice I have found
My griefe is like my love, beyond all bound.

Enter PUTIFER.

PUTIFER.   My servant, maister *Caqueteur* desires to visite you.

CRISPINELLA.   For griefes sake keepe him out, his discourse is   20
like the long word, *Honorificabilitudinitatibus*, a great deale of
sound and no sence: his companie is like a parenthesis to a
discourse, you may admit it, or leav it out, it makes no matter.

Enter FREEVILL *in his disguise.*

FREEVILL.   By your leave sweet creatures.

CRISPINELLA.   Sir, all I can yet say of you, is, you are uncivill.   25

FREEVILL.   You must denie it: By your sorrowes leave,
I bring some musicke, to make sweet your griefe.

V. II. 12 false] Q^c; falce Q^u.   14 lost? Q^c; ~ ∧ Q^u.
23 S.D. *disguise*] 1633; *discourse* Q.

BEATRICE.   What ere you please: O breake my hart
Canst thou yet pant? O dost thou yet survive?
Thou didst not love him, if thou now canst live.   30
FREEVILL *sings,*

> *O Love, how strangely sweet*
> *are thy weake Passions,*
> *That love and joy should meete*
> *in selfe same fashions.*
> *O who can tell*   35
> *the cause why this should move?*
> *But onely this,*
> *no reason, aske of Love.*

BEATRICE *sounds.*

CRISPINELLA.   Hold, peace, the gentlest soule is sowned, O my
best sister.   40
FREEVILL.   Ha, get you gone, close the dores: My *Beatrice,*

Discovers himselfe.

Curst be my indiscreet trials: O my immeasureablie loving.
CRISPINELLA.   She stirs, give aire, she breathes.
BEATRICE.   Where am I, ha? How have I slipt off life?
Am I in heaven? O my Lord, though not loving   45
By our eternall being, yet give me leave
To rest by thie dear side: am I not in heaven?
FREEVILL.   O eternallie much loved, recollect your spirits.
BEATRICE.   Ha, you do speake, I do see you, I do live,
I would not die now: Let me not burst with wonder.   50
FREEVILL.   Call up your bloode, I live to honor you,
As the admired glorie of your sex.
Nor ever hath my love bin false to you,
Onely I presum'd to try your faith too much,
For which I most am grieved.   55
CRISPINELLA.   Brother, I must be plaine with you, you have
wrong'd us.
⟨FREEVILL.⟩   I am not so Covetous to deny it,

30 S.D. *Freevill sings*] *In* Q "Freevill" *follows line* 30 *and the ensuing* S.D. *reads:*
"*He sings, she sounds.*"; "*she sounds*" *here follows* 38 *as* "*Beatrice sounds*".
48 loved] 1633; laued Q.   57 FREEVILL.] 1633; *omitted in* Q.

But yet when my discourse hath staide your quaking,
You will be smoother lipt: and the delight
And satisfaction which we all have got,   60
Under these strange disguisings, when you know,
You will be milde and quiet, forget at last,
"It is much joy to thinke on sorrowes past.
BEATRICE. Do you then live? And are you not untrue?
Let me not die with Joy, pleasure's more extream   65
Then greefe, thers nothing sweet to man but meane.
FREEVILL. Heaven cannot be too gratious to such goodnesse,
I shall discourse to you the several chances, but harke I must yet
rest disguisd, the sudden close of many drifts now meet,

⟨*Assumes disguise again.*⟩

"Where pleasure hath some profit, art is sweet.   70

Enter TYSEFEW.

TYSEFEW. Newes, newes, newes, newes.
CRISPINELLA. Oysters, Oysters, oysters, oysters.
TYSEFEW. Why, is not this well now? Is not this better then
louring, and pouting, and puling, which is hateful to the living,
and vaine to the dead? Come, come, you must live by the quicke, 75
when all is done, and for my owne part, let my wife laugh at me
when I am dead, so sheele smile upon me whilst I live. But to see
a woman whine, and yet keepe her eies drye: mourne, and yet
keepe her cheekes fat: nay, to see a woman claw her husbande
by the feete when he is dead, that would have scratcht him by   80
the face when he was living: this now is somewhat rediculous.
CRISPINELLA. Lord how you prate.
TYSEFEW. And yet I was afraide ifaith that I should ha seene a
Garland on this beauties herse, but time, truth, experience, and
varietie, are great doers with women.   85
CRISPINELLA. But whats the newes? The newes I pray you?
TYSEFEW. I pray you? Nere pray me: for by your leave you may
command me. This tis: the publique sessions which this day is
past, hath doom'd to death ill fortun'd *Malheureux*.
CRISPINELLA. But sir, we heard he offered to make good,   90
That *Freevill* liv'd at Shatews the Jewellers.

65 pleasure's] Q^c; pleasures Q^u.   77 live. But] liue, but Q.

BEATRICE.   And that twas but a plot betwixt them two.

TYSEFEW.   O I, I, he gagd his life with it, but know
    When all approcht the test, Shatewe denide
    He saw or heard of any such complot,   95
    Or of *Freevill*: so that his owne defence,
    Appeard so false, that like a madmans sword,
    He stroke his owne hart. He hath the course of law
    And instantly must suffer: but the Jest
    (If hanging be a jest, as many make it)   100
    Is to take notice of one *Mulligrub*, a sharking vintner.

FREEVILL.   What of him Sir?

TYSEFEW.   Nothing but hanging, the Whoresone slave is mad
    before he hath lost his sences.

FREEVILL.   Was his fact cleere and made aparent Sir?   105

TYSEFEW.   No faith suspitions, for twas thus protested
    A cloke was stolne, that cloke he had, he had it
    Himselfe confest by force, the rest of his defence
    The choller of a Justice wrongd in wine,
    Joynd with malignance of some hastie Jurors,   110
    Whose wit was lighted by the Justice nose, The knave was cast.
    But Lord to heare his mone, his praiers, his wishes,
    His zeal ill timde, and his words unpittied,
    Would make a dead man rise and smile,
    Whilst he observed how feare can make men vile.   115

CRISPINELLA.   Shall we go meet the execution?

BEATRICE.   I shall be rulde by you.

TYSEFEW.   By my troth a rare motion, you must hast,
    For male-factors goes like the world upon wheeles.

BEATRICE [*to Freevill*].   Will you man us? You shall be our   120
    guide.

FREEVILL.   I am your servant.

TYSEFEW.   Ha servant? Zounds I am no companion for Pandors,
    you best make him your love.

BEATRICE.   So will I Sir, we must live by the quicke you say.   125

---

94 Shatewe] 1633; Shatews Q.

103 Whoresone] Q^c; Whoresome Q^u.   104 he hath lost] Q^c; he lost Q^u.

120 (*to Freevill*)] *In* Q *follows* "guide" *as dialogue: placed by* WALLEY AND WILSON *after* "us". *In roman in* Q.

124 you] your Q.

TYSEFEW.   Sdeath a vertue, what a damnd things this?
    Whole trust faire faces, teares, and vowes? Sdeath not I,
    She is a woman, that is, she can ly.
CRISPINELLA.   Come, come, turne not a man of time, to make
                                                    al il,
    Whose goodnesse you conceive not, since the worst of chance   130
    Is to crave grace for heedlesse ignorance.

                                                    Exeunt.

                        ⟨SCENE III⟩

                Enter COCLEDEMOY *like a Sargeant.*

COCLEDEMOY.   So, I ha lost my Sergeant in an ecliptique mist,
    drunke, horrible drunke, he is fine: so now will I fit my selfe. I
    hope this habit will do me no harme, I am an honest man already:
    fit, fit, fit as a puncks taile, that serves every body: By this time
    my Vintner thinkes of nothing but hel and sulpher, he farts fire   5
    and brimstone already, hang tostes, the execution approcheth.

Enter SIR LIONELL, SIR HUBERT, MALHEUREUX *piniond,*
    TYSEFEW, BEATRICE, FREEVILL, CRISPINELLA, FRAN-
    CISCHINA, *and Holberds.*

MALHEUREUX.   I do not blush, although condemnd by lawes,
    No kind of death is shamefull but the cause:
    Which I do know is none, and yet my lust
    Hath made the one (although not cause) most just.   10
    May I not be reprived? *Freevill* is but mislodgd,
    Some lethargie hath seazd him, no, much mallice.
    Do not lay bloud upon your soules with good intents,
    Men may do ill and law sometime repents.

        COCLEDEMOY *picks* MALHEUREUX'S *pocket of his purse.*

SIR LIONELL.   Sir, sir, prepare, vaine is all lewd defence.   15
MALHEUREUX.   "Conscience was law: but now lawes Con-
                                                    science,
    My endles peace is made, and to the poore,
    My purse! My purse!

COCLEDEMOY.   I Sir, and it shall please you the poore has your
purse already.   20

MALHEUREUX.   You are a Wily man.
But now thou sourse of Devils, Oh how I lothe
The very memory of that I adorde!
He thats of faire bloud, well meand, of good breeding,
Best fam'd, of sweet acquaintance and true friends,   25
And would with desperate Impudence loose all these,
And hazard landing at this fatall shore,
Let him nere kill, nor steale, but love a Whore.

FRANCISCHINA.   De man dose rave, tinck a got, tinck a got,
and bid de flesh, de world, and the dible farewell.   30

MALHEUREUX.   Farewell.

                                        FREEVILL *discovers himselfe.*

FREEVILL.   Farewell.

FRANCISCHINA.   Vat ist you sea, ha?

FREEVILL.   Sir your pardon, with my this defence,
Do not forget protested violence   35
Of your low affections; no requests,
No arguments of reason, no knowne danger,
No assured wicked bloodines,
Could draw your hart from this damnation.

MALHEUREUX.   Why staie.   40

FRANCISCHINA.   Unprosperous Divell, vat sall me do now?

FREEVILL.   Therefore to force you from the truer danger,
I wrought the fained, suffering this faire Devil,
In shape of woman to make good her plot,
And knowing that the hooke was deeply fast,   45
I gave her line at will, till with her owne vaine strivings,
See here shees tired: O thou comely damnation!
Doest think that vice is not to be withstood,
O what is woman meerely made of bloud?

SIR LIONELL.   You maze us all, let us not be lost in darknesse!   50

FREEVILL.   All shall be lighted, but this time and place
Forbids longer speech, onlie what you can thinke
Has bin extreamlie ill, is onelie hers.

v. iii. 21 Wily man.] BULLEN; Welyman, Q.   32 and 33 *One line in* Q.
          44 shape] HALLIWELL; shaps Q.

SIR LIONELL.   To severest prison with her, with what hart
                                                    canst live?
   What eies behold a face?   55
FRANCISCHINA.   Ick vil not speake, torture, torture your fill,
   For me am worse then hangd, me ha lost my will.

                        Exit FRANCISCHINA *with the guard.*

SIR LIONELL.   To the extreamest whip and Jaile.
FREEVILL.   Frolique, how is it Sir?
MALHEUREUX.   I am my selfe, how long wast ere I could   60
   Perswade my passion to grow calme to you?
   Rich sence makes good bad language, and a friend
   Should waigh no action, but the actions end.
   I am now worthie yours, when before
   The beast of man, loose bloud distemperd us,   65
   "He that lust rules cannot be vertuous.

Enter MULLIGRUB, MRS MULLIGRUB *and officers.*

OFFICER.   On afore there, roome for the prisoners!
MULLIGRUB.   I praie you do not lead me to execution through
   Cheapeside, I owe M. *Burnish* the gold-smith monie, and I feare
   heele set a Serjant on my backe for it.   70
COCLEDEMOY.   Trouble not your skonce my Christian
   Brothers, but have an eie unto the maine chance, I will warrant
   your shouldiers, as for your necke *Plinius Secundus*, or *Marcus
   Tullius Cycero*, or somebodie it is saies, that a three foulde corde
   is hardlie broken.   75
MULLIGRUB.   Wel, I am not the first honest man that hath bin
   cast away, and I hope shall not be the last.
COCLEDEMOY.   O sir, have a good stomach and mawes, you
   shall have a joyfull supper.
MULLIGRUB.   In troth I have no stomach to it, and it please you 80
   take my trencher, I use to fast at nights.
MRS MULLIGRUB.   O husband, I little thought you should have
   come to think on God thus soon: nay and you had bin hangd
   deservedly, it would never have greevd me, I have known of
   many honest innocent men have bin hangd deservedly, but to   85
   be cast away for nothing.

          59 Sir] WALLEY AND WILSON; Sirs Q.

COCLEDEMOY. Good woman hold your peace, your prittles
and prattles, your bibbles and your babbles, for I pray you
heare mee in private. I am a widdower, and you are almost a
widdow, shal I be welcom to your houses, to your tables, and   90
your other things?

MRS MULLIGRUB. I have a peece of mutton and a featherbed
for you at all times, I pray make hast.

MULLIGRUB. I do here make my confession, if I owe anie man
anie thing, I do hartilie forgive him: if any man owe me anie   95
thing, let him paie my wife.

COCLEDEMOY. I will looke to your wives paiment I warrant
you.

MULLIGRUB. And now good yoke-fellow leave thy poor *Mulligrub.*   100

MRS MULLIGRUB. Naie then I were unkind yfaith, I will not
leave you untill I have seene you hang.

COCLEDEMOY. But brothers, brothers, you must thinke of your
sins and iniquities, you have bin a brocher of prophane vessels,
you have made us drinke of the juice of the whore of *Babylon*,   105
for whereas good ale, *Perrys, Bragets, Syders,* and *metheglins,*
was the true auntient *British* and *Troyan* drinks, you ha brought
in *Popish* wines, *Spanish* wines, *French* wines, *tam marti quam
mercurio,* both *muscadine* and *malmsey,* to the subversion, stag-
gering, and sometimes overthrow of manie a good Christian: 110
You ha bin a great Jumbler, O remember the sins of your nights,
for your night works ha bin unsavorie in the tast of your
Customers.

MULLIGRUB. I confesse, I confesse, and I forgive as I would be
forgiven. Do you know one *Cocledemoy?*   115

COCLEDEMOY. O verie wel: know him? An honest man he is
and a comly, an upright dealer with his neighbours, and their
wives speake good things of him.

MULLIGRUB. Wel, whersoere he is, or whatsoere he is, Ile take
it on my death hees the cause of my hanging, I hartily forgive   120
him, and if he would come forth he might save me, for he only
knowes the why, and the wherfore.

COCLEDEMOY. You do from your harts, and midrifs, and
intrales forgive him then, you wil not let him rot in rusty Irons,

106 *Bragets, Syders*] Q^c; *Bragoes, Syder* Q^u.

procure him to be hangd in lowsie linnen without a song, and　125
after he is dead pisse on his grave?

MULLIGRUB. That hard hart of mine has procurd all this, but I
forgive as I would be forgiven.

COCLEDEMOY. Hang tosts my Worshipfull *Mulligrub*! Behold
thy *Cocledemoy*, my fine vintner, my catastrophonicall fine boy:　130
behold and see.

⟨*Reveals himself.*⟩

TYSEFEW. Blisse, a the blessed, who would but look for 2.
knaves here?

COCLEDEMOY. No knave worshipfull friend, no knave, for
observe honest *Cocledemoy* restores whatsoever he has got, to　135
make you know, that whatsoere he has don, has bin only
Euphoniæ gratia, for Wits sake: I acquit this Vintner as he has
acquitted me, all has bin done for *Emphises* of wit my fine boie,
my worshipfull friends.

TYSEFEW. Goe you are a flattring knave.　140

COCLEDEMOY. I am so, tis a good thriving trade, it coms
forward better then the 7. liberal Sciences, or the nine cardinall
vertues, whiche may well appeare in this, you shall never have
flattering knave turn *courtyer*: and yet I have read of many
Courtyers that have turned flattring knaves.　145

SIR HUBERT. Wast even but so, why then als well?

MULLIGRUB. I could even weepe for joy.

MRS MULLIGRUB. I could weep to, but God knowes for what.

TYSEFEW. Heres another tack to be given, your son and
daughter.　150

SIR HUBERT. Ist possible, hart I, al my hart, wil you be ioyned
here?

TYSEFEW. Yes faith father, marriage and hanging are spun both
in one houre.

126 and 127 *Run on in* Q.
129 Worshipfull *Mulligrub*! Behold] Worsh. *mulli.* behold Q.
130 catastrophonicall] catastrophomicall Q.
134 worshipfull] worsh. Q.
137 *Euphoniæ*] Q^c; *Euphomæ* Q^u.
144 *courtyer*] Q^c; *courtyers* Q^u.
149 Heres] Hers Q.

COCLEDEMOY. Why then my worshipfull good friends I bid my   155
selfe most hartily welcome to your merry nuptials, and wanton
Jigga-joggies. And now my verie fine *Heliconian* Gallantes, and
you my Worshipfull friends in the middle Region:
If with content our hurtlesse mirth hath bin,
Let your pleasd minds as our much care hath bin: 160
For he shall find that slights such triviall wit,
Tis easier to reprove then better it:
We scorne to feare, and yet we feare to swell,
We do not hope tis best: tis all, if Well.

Exeunt.

FINIS

155 worshipfull] worsh. Q.
158 Worshipfull] Worsh. Q.
FINIS] *run on, with Exeunt, to* 164 *in* Q.

TEXTUAL NOTES

SIGLA

Q=Quarto 1605; Qᵘ=Quarto 1605 (uncorrected); Qᶜ=Quarto 1605 (corrected).

1633=Quarto 1633.

BRERETON=J. Le Gay Brereton, *Elizabethan Drama: Notes and Studies.* Sydney 1909.

BULLEN=*The Works of John Marston,* ed. A. H. Bullen. London 1887.

HALLIWELL=*The Works of John Marston,* ed. J. O. Halliwell [-Phillipps.] London, 1856.

WALLEY AND WILSON=*Early Seventeenth Century Plays 1600–42,* ed. H. R. Walley and J. H. Wilson. New York (Harcourt) 1930.

WINE=*The Dutch Courtesan,* ed. M. L. Wine. London (Edward Arnold) 1965.

Prologue

8   delight.] ~, Q.

I. I

S.D.   3.] 3: Q.
21   Harper] Qᶜ; Harp er Qᵘ.
31   Harper‸] ~, Q.
35   followes:] ~, : Q.
55   Sir.] ~, Q.
57   torch!] ~, Q.
58   both. On boy!] both, on boy. Q.
83   Curtezan?] ~. Q.
102   occupation.] ~: Q.
106   home?] ~. Q.
109   up?] vp: Q.
110   case?] ~: Q.

D

121   do ye] Qᶜ; doe ye Qᵘ.
121   they'le] Qᶜ; thy'le Qᵘ.
131   woman;] ~, Q.
137   beauty,] ~‸ Q.
150   prostitution?] ~, Q.

I. II

1   *Mary,*] Mary, Q.
13   Baud?] ~, Q.
22   thee:] ~‸ Q.
24   *lotium*] Qᶜ; lotinu Qᵘ.
25   I,] Qᶜ; ~‸ Qᵘ.
30   worshipfull] worshipfnll Q.
38   by] hy Q.
38   *wa, ha, ho,*] Qᶜ; wa, ha, ho, Qᵘ.
46   rising.] ~, Q.

64   him.] ∼, Q.
65   recreation?] ∼. Q.
72   foole.] ∼, Q.
74   and] aud Q.
85   so.] ∼, Q.
86   entertainement? ∼, Q.
95   beauties?] ∼. Q.
100 names.] ∼, Q.
100 coockold?] ∼, Q.
101 livery.] ∼, Q.
101 foole?] ∼, Q.
102 weake.] ∼, Q.
102 pocky?] ∼, Q.
103 skab.] ∼, Q.
117 prickle,] ∼. Q.
119 old.] ∼, Q.
130 *Wha, ha, ho,*] Wha, ha, ho, Q.
132 good?] ∼. Q.
139 caught.] ∼, Q.
140 her:] ∼ₐ Q.
142 best.] ∼, Q.
151 time?] ∼. Q.
152 me.] ∼ₐ Q.
163 out] Qᶜ; ont Qᵘ.

II. I

8 S.D. *Cantat.*] Cantat. Q.
10   you.] ∼, Q.
16   expresse,] ∼. Q.
17   hart,] ∼. Q.
23   wrongₐ] Qᶜ; ∼, Qᵘ.
25   moove.] mooue, Q.
32   faire;] Qᶜ; ∼ₐ Qᵘ.
32   others] Qᶜ; otheers Qᵘ.
33   seeme.] ∼, Q.
34   ostent,] ∼ₐ Q.
36   brest.] ∼, Q.
44   not feare] Qᶜ; notfeɐre Qᵘ.
53   thee,] Qᶜ; ∼ₐ Qᵘ.
53   me.] ∼, Q.
54   sleightₐ] Qᶜ; ∼: Qᵘ.
58   servant.] seruant, Q.
66   love.] loueₐ Q.
67   Thus] thus Q.
72   name.] ∼, Q.
78   *O*] (*o* Q.

80   unnaturall.] vnnaturall, Q.
81   Snowe.] ∼, Q.
82   me!] ∼ₐ Q.
83   to!] ∼ₐ Q.
90   strumpets?] ∼ₐ Q.
99   of.] ∼, Q.
101 Divells.] Diuellsₐ Q.
113 fearefull] fearefnll Q.
114 affection.] ∼, Q.
120 Incontinence] InContinence Q.
129 errors.] ∼ₐ Q.
143 *Domine!*] ∼. Q.
153 grace!] ∼, Q.
162 Surgeon?] ∼. Q.
164 knave!] ∼, Q.
167 Ti's] Ti,s Q.
168 belong?] ∼, Q.
170 *Rains-cure*] *Raiuscure* Q.
179 well.] ∼, Q.
185 Good] good Q.
192 dwell?] ∼. Q.
196 humor.] ∼, Q.
200 long?] ∼. Q.
201 man.] ∼, Q.
204 pewter.] ∼, Q.
206 disguise.] ∼, Q.
207 Spanish,] ∼ₐ Q.
207 Barbar,] ∼ₐ Q.
208 well.] ∼, Q.
210 breastes] breasteɹ Q.

II. II

S.D. *Loose,*] ∼ₐ Q.
11   daughter!] ∼, Q.
12   done!] ∼, Q.
13   me!] ∼, Q.
26   thee.] ∼ , Q.
32   defie] defiie Q.
32   creature?] ∼. Q.
38   woman] wowan Q.
39   now?] ∼, Q.
45 S.D. *Enter*] *Euter* Q.
79   *Subboys*] *Snbboys* Q.
94   hart.] ∼ₐ Q.
94   stay?] ∼. Q.
121 you?] ∼, Q.

122 can] cau Q.
130 me?] ∼. Q.
143 Well?] ∼. Q.
145 So?] ∼. Q.
152 houre I] Qᶜ; houreI Qᵘ.
159 all men] al lmen Q.
171 affectes.] ∼, Q.
181 not] uot Q.
184 me,] ∼. Q.
188 al's] Al's Q.
195 Farewell.] ∼, Q.
195 revenge∧] ∼, Q.
200 S.D. *Exuent*] *Exit* Q.
203 *He spits*] in r. h. margin in Q.
with space left between "wormes"
and "or".
203 nothing]. ∼, Q.
218 grow.] ∼, Q.
221 feare∧] ∼. Q.
226 wise.] ∼, Q.

II. III

S.D. *Mistresse*] Qᶜ; ∼, Qᵘ.
15 *Andrew?*] *Androw.* Q.
17 Parson.] ∼, Q.
23 quickly.] ∼, Q.
25 will.] ∼, Q.
26 *Andrew?*] ∼. Q.
35–6 this, Ile acquaintance yee] Qᶜ
(some copies); this, Ile
acquaint ance yee Qᵘ; this, Ile
acquaintance yee Qᶜ (some
copies).
36 S.D. *bag*] Qᶜ; *b ag* Qᵘ.
44 the] Qᶜ; th Qᵘ.
45 de-] Qᶜ; de∧ Qᵘ.
57 newes?] ∼, Q.
61 25.] 25, Q.
67 once?] Qᶜ; ∼. Qᵘ.
72 you.] ∼, Q.
74 *Cocledemoy*] *Gocledemoy* (*Huntington Copy only*).
77 *Andrew?*] ∼, Q.
78 towne?] ∼, Q.
79 him.] ∼, Q.
79 *Andrew?*] ∼, Q.

82 wife,] ∼∧ Q.
92 HOLIFERNES.] *Hholof:* Qᵘ;
Holof: Qᶜ.
109 ∧ti's but] .ti's bnt Qᵘ; .ti's but
Qᶜ.

III. I

11 Boddy∧] ∼, Q.
11 beautie,] ∼∧ Q.
19 us,] vs∧ Q.
19 teeth∧] ∼, Q.
32 procreation,] ∼∧ Q.
34 privately.] priuately, Q.
36 complement.] ∼, Q.
39 good.] ∼, Q.
47 Fye, Fye,] ∼, ∼,, Q.
51 nothing.] ∼, Q.
66 flesh.] ∼, Q.
67 in] Qᶜ; *in* Qᵘ.
68 him.] ∼, Q.
74 married,] ∼∧ Q.
74 above,] aboue∧ Q.
75 a] A Q.
77 hould.] ∼, Q.
86 marriage.] ∼, Q.
93 lip,] Qᶜ; ∼∧ Qᵘ.
95 life?] ∼. Q.
103 chopines?] ∼. Q.
123 Caesar] Ceasar Q.
152 give?] giue∧ Q.
157 sure] Qᶜ; surc Qᵘ.
164 servant.] seruant, Q.
182 Contraries?] ∼. Q.
186 And] Aud Q.
191 neere] Qᶜ; neare Qᵘ.
210 so] So Q.
217 What] what Q.
221 man] men Q.
223 love?] loue. Q.
228 you] You Q.
233 women.] ∼, Q.
244 it. Marke.] it marke, Q.
254 Will] NVill Qᵘ; VVill Qᶜ.

III. II

26 shaved?] shaued∧ Q.
31 yet.] ∼, Q.

33   out.] ~, Q.
34   repine.] ~, Q.
39   elements, *Mulligrub.*] ~. ~, Q.
43   vertue] Q^c; verrue Q^u.

III. III

16   Taverne.] Tauerne, Q.
24   thankes.] ~, Q.
29   anone.] ~ ͚ Q.

III. IV

5   love.] loue: Q.
17   Parlour?] ~. Q.
20   strange.] ~? Q.
24   hand?] ~. Q.
30   Salmon?] ~. Q.
35   me?] me. Q.
39   backe?] ~: Q.
65   *Fowtra.*] ~, Q.
67   *Roger!*] ~? Q.
81   monch.] ~͚ Q.
84   about] about about Q.
94   Whether?] ~, Q.
95   it!] ~? Q.
96   so?] so. Q.
101 Goldsmithes?] ~. Q.
104 me.] ~, Q.
105 see?] ~. Q.

IV. I

16   deare] dearc Q.
31   banquet?] ~. Q.
35   necessary.] ~, Q.
38   if] If Q.
38   wee] Wee Q.
40   us.] vs, Q.
55   hart] Hart Q.
77   I!] ~? Q.
90 s.d.   *Exeunt] Exit* Q.

IV. II

2   bloud.] ~: Q.
9   Discipline,] ~. Q.

19   it] It Q.
20   firme.] ~, Q.
22   me?] ~. Q.
22   seizd.] ~, Q.
23   being?] ~. Q.
32   woman's] womna's Q.
37   into.] ~, Q.
40   knave.] knaue ͚ Q.
49   assignd.] assingd. Q.

IV. III

s.d.   *leading*] Q^c; *leadiug* Q^u.
1   *who who ho,*] who who ho, Q.
8   manuscript.] ~͚ Q.
19   gone.] ~, Q.
26   arme.] ~͚ Q.
42   presantly.] ~, Q.

IV. IV

s.d.   LIONELL,] *Lyonell* ͚ Q.
13   *Crispinella*] Crisp. Q.
16   your] Q^c; yous Q^u.
27   me?] Q^c; ~. Q^u.
28   me?] ~, Q.
30   fortnight?] Q^c; ~. Q^u.
31   *Crispinella*] Cris. Q.
32   *Crispinella*] Crisp. Q.
35   but] But Q.
54   affected!] ~? Q.
59   vid most] vidmost Q.
73   set] Set Q.
77   his,] Q^c; ~͚ Q^u.
80 s.d.   *Exeunt.] Exit.* Q.

IV. V

s.d.   TYSEFEW] *Tyssefur* Q^u; *Tyssefue* Q^c.
3   tis] Tis Q.

IV. VI

6   die!] ~? Q.
9   Fraile-Hall!] ~? Q.
11 s.d.   *Exit* ͚] *Exit.* Q.

IV. VII

4   devil.] deuil, Q.
4   nose.] ~, Q.
6   but] But Q.
11   Smithes] smithes Q.
22   wicked] Wicked Q.
24   violence?] ~, Q.
31   you!] ~, Q.
36   asse?] ~, Q.
40   wealth_∧] ~, Q.
43   there?] ~: Q.
43   ho!] ~: Q.
45   hangd?] ~, Q.
47 S.D.   *Enter*] *Euter* Q.
50   *Wha, ha, ha, ho,*] Wha, ha, ha, ho, Q.
53   *Wo, ho, ho, ho.*] Wo, ho, ho, ho, Q.
54   fiddle] Fiddle Q.
67   discerne] Discerne Q.
79   the Watch] *begins line* 80 *in* Q.
93   him!] ~: Q.
93   Constable] Const. Q.
96   Cut-purses,] Qᶜ; ~_∧ Qᵘ.
98   weele] Weele Q.
105 am!] ~? Q.
112 *wha, ha, ha;*] wha, ha_∧ ha, Q.

V. I

S.D. TYSEFEW] *Tissefeue* Qᵘ; *Tissefeu* Qᶜ.
4   you;] ~, Q.
36   What,] ~_∧ Q.
36   your] Qᶜ; yous Qᵘ.
39   pre de tel] Qᶜ; prede tell Qᵘ.
49   monsterous!] ~? Q.
50   Villaine!] ~? Q.
53   error] errors Q.
64   Farewell.] *Farewell. and placed to right as* S.D. Q.
69   hellish!] ~? Q.
71   Man,] ~: Q.
72   bed,] ~: Q.
79   *Cataracks*] Cataracks Qᵘ; Cataracks Qᶜ.

80   sence,] ~_∧ Q.
80   vile_∧] ~, Q.
87   sing.] ~, Q.
88   *Don Dubon*] Qᶜ; Don Dubon Qᵘ.
88   Mestres] Qᶜ; Mestre Qᵘ.
101 creature!] ~? Q.
103 servan,] Qᶜ; ~_∧ Qᵘ.
104 woman!] ~? Q.

V. II

12   and] And Q.
19   *Caqueteur*] Cacature Q.
21   of] Of Q.
22   parenthesis_∧] ~, Q.
22   to] To Q.
23   discourse,] ~_∧ Q.
29   survive?] suruiue. Q.
65   extream] Qᶜ; extreame Qᵘ.
78   whine] Whine Q.
98   hart.] ~, Q.
100 jest,] iest) Q.
102 Sir?] ~. Q.
109 choller] Qᶜ; chollor Qᵘ.
111 cast.] ~, Q.
113 zeal ill timde] Qᶜ; zeale ill timd Qᵘ.
120 us?] ~, Q.
123 Pandors] Qᶜ; pandors Qᵘ.
127 vowes?] ~, Q.
129 time,] Qᶜ; ~_∧ Qᵘ.
129 al] Qᶜ; all Qᵘ.

V. III

2   selfe.] ~, Q.
6 S.D.   LIONELL,] *Lyonell:* Q.
6 S.D.   CRISPINELLA,] *Crisp.* Q.
12   mallice.] ~, Q.
18   purse! My purse!] purse, my purse. Q.
23   adorde!] ~, Q.
36   affections;] ~_∧ Q.
37   danger,] ~. Q.

41 now?] ~. Q.
47 damnation!] ~? Q.
49 bloud?] ~. Q.
50 darkenesse!] ~? Q.
53 ill,] Q^c; ~$_\wedge$ Q^u.
64 now] uow Q.
66 S.D. MULLIGRUB, MRS] *Mulle-
      grub*$_\wedge$ *mistris* Q.
67 prisoners!] ~? Q.
69 Cheapeside] cheapeside Q.
73 *Secundus*] *secundus* Q.
73 *Marcus*] *marcus* Q.

77 shall] Q^c; shal Q^u.
81 trencher,] ~$_\wedge$ Q.
89 private.] priuate, Q.
91 things?] ~. Q.
99 poor] Q^c; pore Q^u.
115 forgiven.] forgiuē, Q.
126 grave?] graue. Q.
134 friend,] Q^c; ~$_\wedge$ Q^u.
153 Yes] yes Q.
155 COCLEDEMOY] *Coele.* Q^u;
      Cocle. Q^c.
157 Jigga-joggies.] Iigga-ioggies$_\wedge$ Q.

COMMENTARY

3–5 the onely end . . . could]
Possibly a backward glance at the
Theatre War in which Marston
and Jonson were ranged on oppo-
site sides. Marston also disclaims
the Horatian and Jonsonian aim of
instructing as well as delighting in
this play (line 8).

DRAMATIS PERSONAE

FAUGH—an expression of disgust;
TYSEFEW—possibly from the
French *tison*, fire-brand, and *feu*,
fire, or from Tisiphone, one of the
Furies; CAQUETEUR—from the
French *caqueter*, to chatter:
MALHEUREUX—from the French
also, a wretched or melancholy
man; COCLEDEMOY'S name suggests cuckoldry—a practice to
which he lays claim; the "mulligrubs" was a fit of depression; and
RAINS-CURE could equally be
Reins-cure. PUTIFER is derived
from *putiferio* (It. = stench, See
Caputi) and it has been noted by
several commentators that Francischina's name is that of a
serving-maid in the commedia
dell'arte.

I. I

Turpe . . . nugas] "It is shameful to
compose difficult trifles," Martial,
Epigrams, 86. The tag superficially

applies to the behaviour of Malheureux (and possibly Freewill,
Cocledemoy and Mulligrub) but
surely self-criticism is intended
here—hence the translation "compose". See Introduction, p. 10.

3–4 sorrowful nose] running nose.

28 have day] have time to pay.

31–32 from . . . wickednesse] (a) in
order not to see evil, (b) as a result
of seeing so much evil. Blind
harpers were common enough to be
proverbial.

35–6 bids . . . them] The blind
harper, not realising the birds have
flown, gets no reward for his
playing and so ironically bids the
dishes and candles "much good
may their (lack of) generosity do
them".

42 *Hic . . . Priami*] "This is the end
of Priam"—though whether Priam
is Mulligrub or Cocledemoy is not
clear. Mulligrub has, in any case,
misquoted *Aeneid* II. 554—*haec
finis Priami fatorum*.

45–6 sinnes of the sellar] Whether
"seller" or "cellar" is not clear—
either sense is applicable to Cocledemoy's description of Mulligrub's sins and iniquities, v. III.
104–13.

68–9 low Countreys] (a) The
Netherlands, (b) the "low" parts
of women (cf. *Comedy of Errors*,
III. II. 143–4). It was English
policy to fight Spain in the Netherlands rather than in England.

70–1 what . . . it] Surely it is better

to let a man have somewhere (or someone) to resort to, even if he suffers the pillory (for having recourse to prostitution).

72 above . . . *Hercules*] beyond restraint by force. Ironically, Hercules symbolised sexual potency as well as strength and virtue. His club he adopted when performing women's duties for Omphale, Queen of Lydia.

75 head sinnes] (*a*) chief sins (*b*) capital offences.

84 courteous one] punning on Courtesan.

86 Publican] punning on public one.

113 onely . . . loose] only men give money that they might (*a*) live loosely, (*b*) lose all they have, financially and sexually.

120–1 quite for quo] one thing in return for another—a confusion of the English "quit" and the Latin *quid pro quo*.

123 *O . . . iustum*] The three nominative forms of the Latin for just or fair—thus, "How fitting is this progression".

131 give . . . fee] pay me my advocate's **fee** for this defence of prostitution.

137–8 since . . . bad] This is drawn from a Neo-Platonic argument that "Beautie is but a faire inne to lodge more fairer guests within", as Ford stated it in *Honour Triumphant* (1606), under the Third Position, *Faire Ladie was never false*. See also Giovanni's argument in *'Tis Pity She's a Whore*, II. v. 14 f, and note also this play, I. II. 126–136.

138–9 *Bonum . . . melius*] a good thing is the better for being shared.

143–4 family of love] here, a brothel. The title was also that of a religious sect to which the Mulligrubs

belong (see III. IV. 5). Mary Faugh claims she is a member of "the family of love" (I. II. 17); she surely means prostitution although some editors read this as the religious sect also. The sect was founded in 1540 by Hendrik Niclaes. It was repressed by Elizabeth and James I and ridiculed by those who interpreted its "love" as licence (*e.g.* III. IV. 9–10).

I. II

8 Restitution is Catholique] possibly, restitution, like the Roman Catholic faith, is forbidden, out of the question,

11 Oracles are seas'd] "Like an oracle you know (are seized of) my meaning" with a pun on ceased.

11 *Tempus preteritum*] the time has passed.

12–13 thou . . . *Temple*] The sacred temple of Diana was burnt down in 356 B.C. by Herostratus and for this impious act the Ionians forbad the mention of his name. The bawd, Mary Faugh, is contrasted with the chaste Diana and likened, as the *ungodly fyer*, to Herostratus.

19 wicked . . . Fridaies] Roman Catholics.

20 Hang toastes] Cocledemoy's exclamation may refer to old toasts—drunkards—or to the small piece of spiced toast dropped into wine.

23–24 supportres . . . drinke] Mary Faugh would provide doctors with business because of the veneral disease she had helped spread. The work of barbers and surgeons was not finally dissociated until 1745.

30 12. Companies] There were twelve "great" livery companies, or trade associations, amongst which were the Drapers and

Goldsmiths but not the Silkmen and Pointmakers.

46–7 rising . . . in-come] Each has a sexual innuendo.

52 *Clearken-well*] a district of London then frequented by prostitutes.

53 *Dixi*] "I have spoken", announcing the completion of a formal speech in Ancient Rome and here standing antithetically to *List then* at I. 29.

60 *Tullies Offices*] *De Officiis* (*On Duties*) by Marcus Tullius Cicero, 44 B.C. It describes a code of behaviour and is addressed to Cicero's son. The first line is given at II. I. 161.

63–4 I will . . . tilt him] Wine reads the corrected original as *stoupe* and glosses it "cup, flagon". *Draw, stoope* and *tilt* are, however, terms from falconry—meaning "entice or lure", "swoop" (at the lure) and "thrust at", respectively.

78–9 what . . . me?] what disturbance of my normal state affects me? The proportion of Malheureux's humours normally makes him cold-blooded; sudden passion (blood) on seeing Francischina upsets this balance. See II. II. 221–6 and III. I. 257.

89 curtian gulfes] from the chasm into which Marcus Curtius leapt, sacrificing himself to save Rome.

98–9 (as . . . Suppositarie] Ariosto (*that worthy spirite*) punned obscenely in Italian on the title of his comedy *I Suppositi* to mean both "the abandoned ones" and "those that can be had" (*Wine*).

111–18 The setting for this song is reproduced by Andrew J. Sabol in "Two Unpublished Stage Songs for the 'Aery of Children' ", *Renaissance News*, XIII (Autumn 1960), 222–32 (*Wine*).

119 Busse] Cf. Herrick: "We busse our wantons but our wives we kisse" (*O.E.D.*).

138 The first of many sententiae. This one is mocked at 155 by Freevill; cf. also 143 and 157; 144 and 159–60; 150 and I. I. 156–58.

161–2 my cast . . . done] the life I have sloughed off must be enlarged to enable you to take it on. In other words, Freevill had no illusions about Francischina whereas the folly of Malheureux excels (*out-thrusts*) that of all men for he argues *'gainst Nature*.

II. I

9 Alwaies . . . love] It is possible that this is not a line of dialogue but the first line of the song that is to be sung here.

57–8 may . . . servant] may you keep your word always.

65 S.D. *The Nitingalls sing*] Wine refers to Bacon's *Sylva Sylvarum*, (1627) which states such a sound was made by a special pipe on the regal (a portable organ) (Century II, 172). Regals were used in plays at least as early as 1565, when they were specified for *Damea and Pythias*. It is possible in this play, however, that the Children of Her Majesty's Revels (by whom the play was performed) sang off-stage, and continued with *sonnets* (*i.e.* love songs).

78 *O miseri . . . habent*] Translated by Florio as: "O miserable they, whose joyes in fault we lay" (*Essays*, III, p. 108).

88 *Diaboli . . . est*] Translated by Florio as "The divels masterpoint lies in our loines, saith S. Jerome", *Essays*, III, p. 86.

109   staines my haviour] inhibits my self-expression.

123   This . . . floore] this argument is more than you can bear.

139   *Absentem . . . putes*] Martial, *Epigrams*, (Loeb xi, lx, 8), translated by Florio: "Of Marble you would thinke she were, / Or that she were not present there." Marston should have written *marmoreamve* and possibly was attracted to the final -*que* by *merumque* in the immediately preceding line of Latin quoted by Montaigne (*Essays*, iii, p. 112).

143   *ut . . . Domine!*] Welcome, Sir!

144   *Ago . . . gratias*] I give you thanks.

161   *Quanquam . . . fili*] Although, Marcus, my son. The opening line of Cicero's *De Officiis* (see note to i. ii. 60).

161–2   does . . . Surgeon?] Cocledomoy is asking Freevill if he needs medical care—presumably for venereal disease. Hence also Reins-cure.

174–5   And . . . have] Possibly from a now lost ballad, "Peggies Complaint for the Death of her Willye" (*Bullen*).

191–2   holde this pawne] possibly some form of security for the shaving gear but much more likely a coin—see 198, *drinke that*.

210   seeme . . . breastes] appear to be innocent.

II. II

3–5   Tho . . . Raine-bow?] Although blue, green and yellow have sexual connotations, the colours here probably do no more than suggest frequent change.

6–7   Cf. ii. i. 101.

29   2. s.] The amount they were willing to pay for a prostitute. (A journeyman earned between about seven shillings and nine shillings a week at this time.)

40   turne Turke] Wine suggests "turn infidel" but Francischina is concerned with the turning of her body, not her soul. Possibly, therefore, "be at anyone's service" (a loose confusion of harem and brothel?).

44   S. *Anthonies* fire] erysipelas.

50–1   no . . . friend] aren't you following the custom of welcoming a guest with a kiss? (For comments on this custom see iii. i. 7 f.)

95   *Video . . . proboque*] O see and approve the better course, followed in Ovid's *Metamorphoses* by *deteriora sequor*, "but take that which is worse".

163   your . . . injoying] the immediate enjoyment of you.

211–4   For . . . heates] Cf. ii. ii. 114–6, 136–7.

II. III

3   as many irons] Cocledemoy will be put into irons weighing 15 lbs (or worth £15?).

5   the losse] of the *neast of goblets* (i. i. 7).

7–9   we do . . . salt butter] The Mulligrubs practices are not in accord with their religious beliefs—those of the Family of Love (see note to i. i. 143–4). What Mrs Mulligrub regards as Protestant, Cocledemoy (v. iii. 108) calls Popish.

11   skore false] overcharge customers by falsely scoring against them drinks they are supposed to have had on credit.

22–3 we . . . trade] *the* trade is not
the cutting of hair, of course, but
conicatching, gulling (see I. I.
47); *polde, shaven,* and *cut* here are all
puns suggesting cheating and so
also *trimd* at 87 and 88 (and see
116) and *dry shaved* at III. III. 37–8.
It is not so much the subtlety of the
wit (or its deficiency) that is
dramatically effective here but the
intimacy with the audience that
Cocledemoy establishes by this use
of language. The closer the
audience and Cocledemoy share his
jokes, the more isolated Mulligrub
becomes, the more his foolish self-
esteem and hypocrisy are exposed,
and the more effective the comedy.

51 *Paris Garden*] Originally a particular place for bear baiting on the
South Bank of the Thames. It was
moved a little to the east and later
the Swan Theatre was built on the
original Paris Garden site in 1595.

68 this bal] ball of soap (cf. III. II.
22–3.)

79–80 one . . . Councell] an alderman of London.

III. I

13–14 standing . . . sarcenet] a
fashionably-dressed man wearing a
high, embroidered collar and
clothes lined with fine silk.

15–16 John a stile] fictitious name
for one of the parties in a legal
action (*O.E.D.*).

16 ploydens face] probably (following *John a stile*) a lawyer's face
after the Tudor lawyer Edmund
Plowden whose name was popular-
ised in the proverb "The Case is
altered, quoth Plowden" (*Tilley*,
CIII). It was often spelt with a
"y" (and Tilley gives three such
examples).

35 nature . . . apparell] "nature as it
is" and also, without a pareil
(equal).

61 broake my skull] troubled my
head. Despite Putifer's efforts, we
are not given the benefit of her
lecture.

74 got . . . above] Echoes line 71.
This passage is packed with sexual
innuendo—thus *horse* (81) means
also whores.

89 would . . . shoulders] make love
to other women.

122 A motion] a subject for dis-
cussion *and* a puppet show. The
titles in 123–4 are all of popular
puppet shows.

169 on the hippe] at a disadvantage—
a wrestling term.

194–5 my . . . backe] Dancing steps;
the *carantapace* is the Coranto.
The sexual implication of *falling
backe* follows on from *service* at
188.

212 *In . . . formas?*) I am inspired to
tell of forms changed anew (the
opening line of Ovid's *Metamorphoses*).

217 *Lindabridis*] A character in *The
First Part of the Mirrour of
Princely deedes and Knighthood,*
1578, by Diego Ortûnez de
Calahorra. The name was at one
time used allusively for a mistress
(so by Scott in *Kenilworth*) but
can only loosely be applied to
Malheureux.

231–3 nothing . . . women] Cf. II. I.
120–2.

III. II

35–7 ten . . . fortnight] this very
meagre product of the parson's
tithe was the result of a lack of
eduction, so giving him little
cause for defecation.

37–8 workes of superarrogation] deeds beyond those necessary for salvation, according to the Roman Catholic Church, and which could be made available to other wretched souls. Cocledemoy states that such deeds as he describes would be so horrendous that not even the good works of others could save him.

39 jumbler of elements] mixer of water with wine (again at V. III. 111).

44–5 beware . . . carts] be careful how you go—ladders to the scaffold have rungs to climb, the noose its knots, and there are tumbrils for transportation to the place of execution (for theft).

III. III

1f Mistress Mulligrub's monologue is full of obvious sexual innuendoes.

8 she paints now] uses make-up—a most reprehensible action and something which, even a century later, Moll Flanders was to claim she did not stoop to doing.

21–2 a peece . . . serves] game in season, but with sexual innuendo, as Cocledemoy maintains at IV. VII 73–6 and see III. IV. 10.

33–4 his . . . side] The suggestion of heraldic arms for Mulligrub is comically incongruous, of course.

III. IV

23 he] presumably Burnish.

54 Good] The 1633 Quarto and some later editors (e.g. Bullen and Wine) not unreasonably emend Good to God, but the mistaking of such an obvious imprecation (though possible) strikes me as strange. Whereas she might well say I trust in God at 61–2, the oath-like

nature of this expression could demand a euphemism appropriate to her religious sect.

85 take . . . sleeves] Sleeves were then often separate from the body of a garment and could be changed at will.

104 Ile . . . you] I'll cuckold you (give you horns).

IV. I

30 A . . . wispe] Possibly either a mere will o' the wisp (i.e. insubstantial), or a figure of straw for a scold to rail at (O.E.D.). Wine suggests an allusion to the proverb "As wise as a wisp".

47 ten . . . bellie) Wine considers this implies Tysefew's freakishness (but is he a freak?) but gestation in humans runs quite normally from 280 days (ten lunar months) to about 300.

51–2 Euphues . . . Lies] Euphues and his England (1580) was Lyly's sequel to his Euphues: the Anatomy of Wit (1578). Palmerin de Oliva is the hero of another high-styled romance; it was translated into English by Anthony Munday. The Legend of Lies is taken to be fictitious—but I wonder if it does not glance ironically at Chaucer's The Legend of Good Women.

60 swalowd flap-dragons] a game in which burning raisins were snatched out of lighted brandy and eaten.

60 stabd armes] pricked the arm to let blood drip into wine before it is drunk. These actions in 59–61 (which are also described at the very end of Middleton's A Trick to Catch the Old One) are all those of a gallant protesting—affirming—his love.

62–3 copper bearde] According to Dekker in *The Gull's Hornbook* Marston had red hair and little legs. One or both of these characteristics is mentioned in seven of his plays (See Gustav Cross, "The Date of *The Malcontent* Once More", *P.Q.*, XXXIX, p. 12, fn. 38).

65 By ( )] The use of empty brackets and similar devices is puzzling. At III. I. 106 "the," indicates an interrupted speech; here and at IV. IV. 17 it is *possible* that an oath has been omitted, but the text is freely spattered with invocations (*e.g. Gods foot* at IV. I. 50–1) and this text is earlier than the Act of 1606 which prohibited profanity on the stage. Possibly the brackets indicate stage business. (Cf. the gap in the original at II. II. 203). Fredson Bowers suggests such brackets are a stage direction (to indicate an indecent movement of the legs) in his note to III. II. 49 of *Patient Grissil* (*The Dramatic Works of Thomas Dekker*, I. 292). At IV. VII. 57 an obvious rhyme word is omitted and this, J. A. B. Somerset has suggested, might be designed to elicit the word from the audience (*The Comic Turn in English Drama, 1470–1616*, p. 471).

74–5 no crumpt . . . mantle] See note to III. I. 89.

79 I . . . morning] As Cockledemoy sings at IV. VII. 51–2: "Maids on their backes, Dreame of sweet smackes."

IV. II

3–4 tane . . . life] had its full effect.

4–5 they . . . quarrell] *force* may mean physical, mental, or moral strength. In view of line 2, the meaning of this passage seems to be "those with the most powerful intellects are most prone to quarrell."

40 knave] Either Cocledemoy (see V. III. 21) or Freevill himself in his disguise as Don Dubon.

48 with side-wind] by indirect means.

IV. III

1 Francke a Franck-hall] Francischina (=Frank—cf. II. I. 151, IV. VI. 8–9) is ironically referred to as mistress of all she surveys like some earlier Toad of Toad Hall.

10–17 The occasional words in English in this gabble, *e.g. goblet* and *Punck rampant* indicate the kind of transaction Cocledemoy is hoping to effect.

26 seetes] sweets (cf. II. II. 47 and 48 and V. I. 23, 27) though Bullen, Wood, and Wine, all read "feet(e)s". The long "s" is, however, quite plain and *sweets* as used by Francischina is rather more to the point than *feets*.

IV. IV

22 cough . . . everlastings] (*a*) eternal coughing, (*b*) a cough that will see him to eternity.

92–3 Were . . . saved] This awkward expression presumably means that even were there three such women as Beatrice in the world, she alone (as *primus inter pares*) could be certain of salvation whilst the other two might (or might not) be saved.

IV. VI

2–3 cupping glasses] Normally used in the operation of letting blood.

Here possibly a wine glass used in conjunction with *stabd armes* (see IV. I. 60 note).

38–9 matter in us scabs] (*a*) pus in such sores, (*b*) sense in scoundrels like we are.

41–2 lets . . . God) Wine takes Mulligrub to be the object of the imperative *let* but Harvey Wood's suggestion is more attractive. Referring to Glapthorne's *Wit in a Constable* (1640) he suggests that the seventeenth century constable "does least harm (if he do no good) when he . . . *sleepes for th' good o' th' Commonwealth*".

48f A similar song (noted by Wood) is to be found in Chapman's *May-Day* (1611), III. I. 125f: "Maids in your smocks / Set open your locks / Down, down, down, / Let chimney-sweeper in / And he will sweep your chimneys clean, / Hey, derry, derry, down." Regarding the omission in line 57, see note to IV. I. 65.

19 S.D. *Cantat . . . cithera*] she sings and dances to the cittern (a lute-like instrument).

88 Metre *Don Dubon*] Freevill.

106 as thee] is as thee.

13 some . . . him] for some other, secret, purpose, has spoken maliciously of him.

82 Lord . . . prate] Crispinella may chide Tysefew but what he says is very much in accord with her own comments on kissing and marriage.

119 male-factors . . . wheeles] the carts of III. II. 45.

125 Echoes Tysefew at 75.

38 No . . . bloodines] As Malheureux quickly rejected the idea of killing Freevill, this seems irrelevant at first sight. Possibly the blood here is that of the humours and thus the meaning—no assurance of the wickedness of his newly-acquired hot blood (=passion, cf. I. II. 78–9 note) could persuade him from associating with Francischina. Cf. also V. III. 65–6.

43 wrought the fained] practised the deception or sham.

47 shees tired] exhausted like a fish that has been played on a line.

74–5 or . . . broken] The *somebodie* is Ecclesiastes at 4.12.

83–6 nay . . . nothing] Cf. Malheureux at V. III. 8. Mistress Mulligrub is like the wife of Socrates who, according to Montaigne in Florio's translation said, "*how unjustly doe these bad judges put him to death! What? Wouldest thou rather they should execute me justly?* replide he to her." (*Essays*, II. p. 300).

103 But . . . brothers] Possibly *brothers* should be in the singular, but Cocledemoy may not only be addressing Mulligrub. He is fond of holding forth and he seems here, in a mock sermon, to be drawing the attention of all to their sins before speaking to Mulligrub of his in particular. Cf. V. III. 71–2.

107 *Troyan*] According to legend, Brute, the great-grandson of Aeneas, founded London after the fall of Troy.

108–9 *tam* . . . *mercurio*] as much for Mars (war) as Mercury (trading or thieving).

109 *muscadine* and *malmsey*] strong, sweet, wines.

124–6 rot . . . grave] See II. III. 3; IV. VI. 5; III. II. 10–11; and IV. VI. 6–7 for the origin of each threat recalled by Cocledemoy. Marston collects them together with commendable accuracy.

137 *Euphoniæ gratia*] for the sake of euphony—so that all shall sound well. It may be that Marston is dismissing Cocledemoy's pranks as no more than verbal humour, yet the relationship between the acts of Cocledemoy, euphony, and wit, is a little awkward. In view of the concern in the main plot for the proper ordering of life—from Malheureux's imbalance to Crispinella on kissing and marriage—it is just possible that Marston

had *oeconomia* in mind rather than *euphonia*. *Oeconomia* is defined by Thomas Cooper in *Thesaurus Linguae Romanae et Britannicae* (London 1573) as "an order in writing or pleading whereby every thing is set in his due place", verbal decorum thus reflecting the proper ordering of life. *Wit* would then be as much wittiness as discretion and wisdom.

142 7. liberal Sciences] grammar, logic, rhetoric (the *trivium*), arithmetic, geometry, music, astronomy (the *quadrivium*).

142–3 nine . . . vertues] There should, of course, be only seven; perhaps Cocledemoy adds wit and euphony!

158 the middle Region] Probably the audience in general rather than any section of it (that is, all between the performers and those outside the theatre?).

BIBLIOGRAPHY

ABBREVIATIONS

E.L.H. = *A Journal of English Literary History.*
J.E.G.P. = *Journal of English and Germanic Philology.*
M.L.R. = *Modern Language Review*
M.P. = *Modern Philology.*
P.M.L.A. = *Publications of the Modern Language Association of America.*
P.Q. = *Philological Quarterly.*
R.E.L. = *A Review of English Literature.*
R.E.S. = *Review of English Studies.*
S.P. = *Studies in Philology.*

I. MARSTON'S WORKS
A. COLLECTED EDITIONS

The Workes. London 1633 (two issues).

The Works of John Marston, ed. J. O. Halliwell [-Phillipps] 3 vols. London 1856.

The Works of John Marston, ed. A. H. Bullen, 3 vols. London 1887.

The Plays of John Marston, ed. H. Harvey Wood, 3 vols. Edinburgh (Oliver and Boyd) 1934–9.

B. *THE DUTCH COURTESAN*

The Dutch Courtesan. First Quarto. London 1605.

The Dutch Courtesan, ed. M. L. Wine. London (Edward Arnold) 1965.

Early Seventeenth Century Plays 1600–42, edd. H. R. Walley and J. H. Wilson. New York (Harcourt) 1930. (Includes *The Dutch Courtesan.*)

II. CRITICAL STUDIES
A. BIBLIOGRAPHICAL

BRETTLE, R. E. "Bibliographical Notes on some Marston Quartos and Early Collected Editions", *The Library* (4th series) VIII (1927) pp. 336–48 and XII (1931) pp. 235–42.

——. "Notes on John Marston: (i) Handwriting, (ii) Life 1605–16", *R.E.S* N.S. XIII (1962) pp. 390–93.

GREG, W. W. *A Bibliography of the English Printed Drama to the Restoration* I and III. London 1939 and 1957.

TANNENBAUM, S. A. *John Marston, A Concise Bibliography*. New York 1940.

B. GENERAL

ALLEN, MORSE S. *The Satire of John Marston*. Columbus 1920 and New York (Haskell House) 1965.

ARONSTEIN, P. "John Marston als Dramatiker", *Englische Studies* XX, pp. 377–9, XXI pp. 28–79 (1895).

AXELRAD, A. JOSE. *Un Malcontent Élizabéthain, John Marston, 1576–1634*. Paris (Didier) 1955.

BRERETON, J. LE G. "John Marston", in *Writings on Elizabethan Drama*. Melbourne (Melbourne U. P.) 1948.

BRETTLE, R. E. "Marston born in Oxfordshire", in *M.L.R.* XXII (1927), pp. 7–14.

——. "John Marston, Dramatist, at Oxford", in *R.E.S.* III (1927), pp. 398–405.

——. "Notes on John Marston: (i) Handwriting (ii) Life 1605–16", in *R.E.S* (N.S.) XIII, (1962), pp. 390–93.

CAMPBELL, O. J. "Shakespeare's Jaques and the Malcontent", in *Huntingdon Library Bulletin*, 1935, pp. 71–102.

CAPUTI, ANTHONY. *John Marston, Satirist*. Ithaca (Cornell) 1961.

CHAMBERS, SIR E. K. *The Elizabethan Stage*, I–IV (esp. III). Oxford (Clarendon Press) 1923.

CLOUGH, W. O. "The Broken English of Foreign Characters of the Elizabethan Stage", in *P.Q.* XII (1933), pp. 255–68.

CRAWFORD, C. *Collectanea, Second Series*. Stratford-on-Avon (Shakespeare Head Press) 1907.

CROSS, K. G. W. "Marston, Montaigne, and Morality: *The Dutch Courtesan* Reconsidered", in *E.L.H.* XXVII (1960), pp. 30–43.

——. "The Date of *The Malcontent* Once More", in *P.Q.* XXXIX (1960), pp. 104–13.

——. "Notes on Marston's Vocabulary", in *Notes and Queries*, 1954 (Oct.); 1955 (Jan., Feb., May, Aug., Oct., Nov.); 1956 (Aug., Nov.); 1957 (Feb., May, July, Dec.); 1958 (Jan., Mar.); 1959 (Mar., Apr., July–Aug., Oct.); 1960 (Apr.); 1961 (Apr., Aug., Oct.); 1963 (Aug.). These notes reveal the full extent of Marston's neologistic habits.

——. "The Retrograde Genius of John Marston", in *R.E.L.*, II (1961), pp. 19–27.

CURRY, JOHN V. *Deception in Elizabethan Comedy*. Chicago (University of Loyola) 1955.

DORAN, MADELEINE. *Endeavours of Art*. Madison (University of Wisconsin) 1954.

ELIOT, T. S. "John Marston", in *Elizabethan Essays*. London (Faber) 1934.

ELLIS-FERMOR, U. M. *The Jacobean Drama*. London (Methuen) 1936.

ELSON, J. J. *The Wits*. Ithaca (Cornell) 1932.

GRAVES, T. S. "Some Aspects of Extemporal Acting", in *S.P.* XIX (1922), pp. 429–56.

HERRICK, MARVIN T. *Tragicomedy*. Illinois (University of Illinois) 1955.

HUGHES, L. AND SCOUTEN, A. H. "Some Theatrical Adaptations of a Picaresque Tale", in *Studies in English* XXVI (1945-6), pp. 98–114.

HUNTER, G. K. "English Folly and Italian Vice: The Moral Landscape of John Marston", in *Jacobean Theatre*, ed. J. R. Brown and Bernard Harris. London (Edward Arnold) 1960.

JACKSON, JAMES J. "Sources of the Subplot of Marston's *The Dutch Courtesan*", in *P.Q.*, XXXI (1952), pp. 223–24.

KOEPPEL, E. *Quellenstudien du den Darmen Ben Jonson's, John Marston's, und Fletcher's*. Erlangen 1895.

O'CONNOR, JOHN J. "The Chief Source of Marston's *Dutch Courtesan*", in *S.P.*, LIV (1957), pp. 509–15.

ORNSTEIN, ROBERT. *The Moral Vision of Jacobean Tragedy*. Madison (University of Wisconsin) 1960.

PELLEGRINI, GUILIANO, *Il Teatro di John Marston*. Pisa (Libreria Goliardica Editrice) 1952.

PETER, J. D. *Complaint and Satire in Early English Literature*. Oxford (Clarendon Press) 1956.

—— "John Marston's Plays", in *Scrutiny*, XVII (1950), pp. 132–53.

PRESSON, ROBERT K. "Marston's *Dutch Courtezan*: The Study of an Attitude in Adaptation", in *J.E.G.P.*, LV (1956), pp. 406–413.

SABOL, ANDREW J. "Two Unpublished Stage Songs for the 'Aery of Children' ", *Renaissance News*, XIII (1960), pp. 222–32.

SAINMONT, J. *Influence de Montaigne sur Marston et Webster*. Louvain 1914.

SCHOENBAUM, S. "The Precarious Balance of John Marston", in *P.M.L.A.*, LXVII (1952), pp. 1069–1078.

SOMERSET, J. A. B. *The Comic Turn in English Drama, 1470–1616*, an unpublished Ph.D. thesis. University of Birmingham 1966.

SPENCER, THEODORE. "John Marston", in *The Criterion* XIII (1934), pp. 581–99.

——. "The Elizabethan Malcontent", in *J. Q. Adams Memorial Studies*. Washington (Folger Library) 1948, pp. 523–35.

STEIN, ARNOLD. "The Second English Satirist", in *M.L.R.* XXXVIII (1943), pp. 273–78.

STOLL, E. E. "Shakspere, Marston, and the Malcontent Type", in *M.P.*, III (1906), pp. 281–303.

SWINBURNE, A. C. *The Age of Shakespeare*. London (Chatto and Windus) 1908.

ZALL, PAUL M. "John Marston, Moralist", in *E.L.H.*, XX (1953), pp. 186–93.

III. OTHER WORKS CITED

BACON, FRANCIS. *Sylva Sylvarum*. London 1627.

DEKKER, THOMAS. *Patient Grissil*, in *The Dramatic Works of Thomas Dekker*, ed. Fredson Bowers, vol. I. Cambridge (Cambridge U.P.) 1953.

JONSON, BEN. *Bartholomew Fair*, in *Ben Jonson*, ed. C. H. Herford and Percy and Evelyn Simpson, vol. VI Oxford (Clarendon Press) 1938.

MONTAIGNE, MICHAEL, LORD OF. *Essays*. London (Everyman) 1910.

GLOSSARY

abhomination	*abomination (by false derivation from* ab homine *instead of* ab omine—cf. *L.L.L.* v. i. 18 f), ii. ii. 126.
a deere leevest	*alderliefest (Dutch for dearest),* ii. ii. 48-9.
aderliver	*alderliefest (Dutch for dearest),* i. ii. 80.
affect	*profess, love,* ii. i. 98.
affects	*desires, affections,* ii. i. 68.
all-fles-Lovers	*all-flesh Lover, lecher,* v. i. 29.
and	*if,* i. ii. 62.
aporne	*apron,* iii. iv. 84.
Apostata	*apostate, renegade,* i. ii. 161.
arsie, varsie	*backside first, back to front,* iii. iv. 6.
as live	*as lief,* iii. i. 21.
Aunt	*bawd,* i. ii. 8.
band	*bond,* ii. i. 96.
barmd	*fermented,* iii. ii. 38.
bate	*bath,* iv. iii. 25.
bellide	*bellied,* i. ii. 3.
belly act	*copulation,* i. ii. 72.
begar	*By God!* iv. iii. 29.
blacke booke	*record of those to be punished,* iv. vii. 97.
Blouze	*trull, wench,* ii. ii. 89.
Bragets	*bragget, an alcholic drink of honey and ale,* v. iii. 106.
Bridewell	*house of correction, prison,* i. ii. 52.
bulchin	*bull-calf,* ii. i. 149.
Bush	*buss, kiss,* v. i. 103.
cack	*defecate,* ii. i. 204.
Cantat	*He or She sings,* ii. i. 8, ii. ii. 53, ii. iii. 81.
capriceous	*humourous, fantastic,* i. ii. 66.
cardes	*playing cards,* ii. i. 209.
carving	*apportioning the blame = settling the dispute,* iv. i. 17.
case	(a) *case,* (b) *kaʒe = pudendum muliebre (Bullen),* i. i. 110.
catafugo	*spitfire (Spanish),* iv. iii. 1.
catastrophonicall	*nonce word (O.E.D.); related to fiest (Wood),* ii. i. 194, v. iii. 130.
caudels, cawdle	*warm drink(s) of gruel and wine,* iii. ii. 40, iv. iii. 33.
chance	*misfortune,* v. ii. 130.
chances	*events,* v. ii. 68.

chopines	*high-heeled shoes worn by fashionable women* (cf. I. II. 93), III. I. 103.
clean	*comely, shapely*, II. I. 151.
clippe	*embrace, hug*, I. II. 82.
close	*hidden, secretely*, IV. II. 39.
Cockatrice	*prostitute (originally, the basilisk)*, I. II. 98.
Cock-stones	*kidney beans (an aphrodisiac, Wine)*, IV. III. 33–4.
cogging	*cheating*, I. I. 6.
common up-taile	*whore*, IV. III. 17.
complot	*plot*, V. II. 95.
conceave	*think*, III. I. 52.
conceaving	*becoming pregnant*, III. I. 53.
conicatching	*deceiving (a coney being a rabbit)*, I. I. 47.
consorted with	*accompanied by*, I. I. 17.
containe	*contain myself*, II. II. 105.
Court misfortune	*pox*, I. I. 108.
covers	(a) *includes*, (b) *copulates*, I. II. 18.
Covetous	*excessively anxious*, V. II. 57.
cozend on't	*cheated of it*, III. IV. 55.
crackers	*fireworks*, IV. VII. 113.
crackt	*flawed, faulty*, I. I. 116.
crosse	*across*, II. I. 79.
cunny	*coney*, III. I. 127.
curious	*skilful, careful*, I. I. 136.
cursey	*curtsey*, III. I. 22.
custom	*usage (including a sexual sense)*, I. II. 132.
cut	(a) *trim the hair*, (b) *have the feelings deeply hurt*, II. III. 24.
cutting	*sharp practice*, II. II. 110.
dayly	(a) *constant*, (b) *in the daytime* I. I. 77.
deathes head	*ring with skull thereon (worn by prostitutes)*, I. II. 49.
defame	*defamation, infamy*, II. I. 87.
delicate	*delightful*, IV. III. 26.
Diaper	*diagonally patterned white linen*, III. IV. 1.
dietie	*deity*, II. I. 47.
disguise with	*conceal from*, I. I. 81.
doubtlesse	*free from doubt*, II. II. 139.
Drawer	*tapster*, I. I. 22.
drifts	*schemes, plots*, V. II. 69.
dry shaved	*cheated*, III. III. 37–8.
dyet drinks	*treatment for venereal disease (cf. regimen)*, I. II. 24.
eager	*brittle*, IV. II. 45.
easie	(a) *slight*, (b) *effortlessly written*, PRO. 1.
ejaculatories	*short prayers*, IV. II. 10.
eld	*old age*, I. II. 143 and 157.
elected	*chosen one*, I. II. 87.

entierly	*sincerely*, III. IV. 77.
even	*fairly*, IV. I. 7.
exspectance	*expectation*, PRO. 15.
extreame	*immoderate*, II. I. 49 and 50.
extreamest	(a) *unsurpassable*, (b) *too excessive*, V. III. 58.
fact	*evil deed, crime*, V. II. 105.
falling in	*love-making*, IV. I. 90.
false fiers	*false alarms*, III. IV. 87.
familiar	*free, intimate*, I. II. 85.
fiest a grace	*break wind* (fist) *freely*, II. I. 153.
Figo	*a fig for you (usually accompanied by a gesture)*, III. IV. 80.
flatte-cappes	*tradesmen*, II. II. 30.
flattes	*dulls*, IV. I. 42.
foolish	*wanton*, IV. I. 33.
Foutra, Fowtra	*an obscenity (cf. 2 Hen. IV*, V. III. 100), II. II. 33, III. IV. 65.
Foyst	(a) *fustiness, smell*, (b) *one who foists something on someone—a cheat*, III. III. 45.
french, the	*venereal disease*, I. I. 123.
french Crowne	(a) *a coin (an Escu)*, (b) *baldness caused by venereal disease*, I. I. 122.
froe	*frow, Dutchwoman*, I. I. 146.
full	*absolute, open*, I. I. 87.
furniture	*equipment*, II. I. 188–9.
gag'd	*pledged*, II. I. 5.
glister	(a) *suppository* (cf. I. II. 99), (b) *glitter*, III. I. 142.
glisterpipe	*clyster pipe, enema syringe*, I. II. 12.
Gonory	*gonorrhoea*, II. I. 131.
good	*financially sound*, III. II. 3.
gossope it	*join in*, III. IV. 86.
Grand Grincome	*venereal disease*, II. II. 6.
grav'd	*engraved*, III. III. 34.
grogaran	*grogram, coarse fabric*, III. II. 35.
growe of	*grow apart, separate*, II. I. 99.
Gudgeon	*small fish, easily caught*, II. I. 184.
hammerd out	*beaten out (so as to be unrecognisable)*, I. I. 7.
handsomly	*carefully*, IV. I. 5.
hard bound	*constipated*, I. II. 70.
haviour	*behaviour*, II. I. 109.
haet	*anger*, IV. IV. 2.
Heliconian	*devoted to the Muses (who lived on Mt Helicon)*, V. III. 157.
Honorificabilitudinitatibus:	*honourableness (the popular "longest word" of the 16th century—cf. L.L.L.* V. I. 44), V. II. 21.
Hospitall	*home for destitute, poor-house*, II. II. 21.

I	*Aye, yes, (passim).*
ill	*unkind,* II. I. 21.
imparlarde	*imparloured (=in the parlour),* I. I. 19.
impropriation	*property (particularly of the Church—and so appropriate in conjunction with the Family of Love),* I. I. 145.
Impudence	*shamelessness,* IV. IV.. 97, V. III. 26.
inhauntres	*associate,* I. II. 23.
inoying	*enjoying,* II. II. 137.
In-step	*part of the foot (but with sexual innuendo),* II. I. 152.
insufficient	*inadequate,* II. I. 109.
jaw-falne	*dejected, crest-fallen,* I. I. 43.
Jole	*jowl, cheek (but especially "head and shoulder" of salmon),* III. III. 31.
Jumbler	*mixer of wine and water,* V. III. 111.
kinde	*natural disposition, descent,* II. I. 91.
large	*fully,* IV. I. 20.
leudlie	*wickedly,* IV. IV. 91.
lewd	*bungling, or perhaps, unprincipled,* V. III. 15.
lotium	*medicine,* I. II. 24; *semen,* I. II. 74.
Lov'd	*Beloved,* I. I. 66.
Mall	*Mary,* III. IV. 80.
man	*escort,* V. II. 120.
Mangonist	*one who furbishes up inferior goods for sale, (O.E.D.),* I. I. 98.
man of time	*time server,* V. II. 129.
mark	*target,* I. I. 24.
Marry	*an exclamation of surprise,* II. II. 91; *wed* II. II. 92.
mawes	*jaws,* V. III. 78.
mayster	*Master, Mr.* III. IV. 94.
meerely	*entirely,* V. III. 49.
mentula	*penis,* IV. III. 4.
mercy	*power to extend or withhold clemency (O.E.D.),* IV. VI. 13.
metheglin	*form of mead (an alchoholic drink made from honey),* V. III. 106.
mettle	(a) *spirit,* (b) *metallic substance,* IV. I. 26.
Mettre	*usually Anglo-Dutch for* Mistress; Mettres *is used at* II. II. 119; Metre *at* V. I. 84, 88, *and* mestre *at* V. I. 84 *mean Master.*
Mischiefe	*source of evil,* V. I. 104.
misgone	*gone astray,* II. II. 219.
Mittimus	*warrant for committal to jail,* IV. VII. 99.
monch	*much, grind down,* III. IV. 81.
money Creature	*prostitute,* I. I. 97.
Mulligrubs	*a fit of depression,* II. I. 163.

Mush at	*Much at!* v. i. 85.
musicke	*musical instruments*, ii. i. sd.
Myn-here, min here:	*mynheer* (*Dutch Master*), v. i. 4, 20.

Naunt	*Aunt, Bawd*, ii. ii. 22.
neast of goblets	*series of interlocking goblets*, i. i. 7.
neck peece	(?) *jowl of salmon*, iii. iv. 64–5.
nice	(?) *difficult to please*, i. ii. 135; *delicate*, ii. i. 12.
nightcaps	*either nocturnal bullies* (*O.E.D.*) *ironically*; *or, men of law* (*Wine*), iv. iv. 34.
Night-railes	*nightwear*, iv. vii. 56.
no question	*doubtless*, ii. i. 101.
now	*present*, pro. 4.
noyse	*musical ensemble*, ii. iii. 63, 113; *music; disturbance*, ii. iii. 84.

Obligation	*bond, promissory note*, iii. ii. sd.
often	*frequent*, ii. i. 40.
only	*uniquely, utterly*, ii. i. 32; *peerless*, ii. i. 40.
or . . . or	*either . . . or*, (*passim*).
ostent	*ostentation*, ii. i. 34.

parcell guilt	*partially gilt* (*e.g. on inside of cup only*), iii. ii. 4.
patiently	*sedulously, carefully*, i. i. 32.
peec'd	*added to*, iii. i. 105.
perdy	*per Dieu, By God*, i. i. 158.
peece of mutton	*prostitute, pudenda*, v. iii. 92.
polde	(a) *cut hair off*, (b) *robbed*, ii. iii. 22.
politike	*expedient*, ii. i. 70.
pomatum	*ointment*, iii. i. 17.
poyntmaker	*maker of points* (*laces for fastening clothing*), i. ii. 32.
precise	(a) *strict*, (b) *Puritan*, iv. ii. 46.
preposterously	*pre-posterior-ously—bottom first*, i. i. 34.
presently	*at once*, (*passim*).
prise	*prize*, iii. i. 68.
privie	(a) *secret*, (b) *latrine*, (c) *privates;* ii. iii. 59.
prophane vessels	(a) *wine casks*, (b) *prostitutes*, v. iii. 104.
protest	*proclaim*, ii. i. 256.
protested	*declared*, ii. i. 17, v. iii. 35.
pumpes	*light shoes*, iii. i. 206.
puncke	*prostitute*, ii. ii. 81.

quicke	*living*, v. ii. 75, 125.

ranke	*take places* (*for dancing*), iv. i. 5.
receipt	*place for receiving stolen goods*, iv. vii. 96.
recreation	*pleasure* (*with sexual implication*), i. ii. 65.
rheume	(a) *cold*, (b) *venereal disease*. ii. ii. 64 and 65.
rhewme	*watering*, iii. ii. 32.

Rosa Solis	*a cordial (originally from juice of sundew, later spiced brandy)*, II. III. 106–7.
Rotten	*infected with venereal disease*, I. II. 3.
sallow	*swallow*, V. I. 30.
Sarpego	*spreading skin disease (especially ringworm, but here venereal)*, II. I. 131.
say	(a) *fine cloth*, (b) *what is said in a message*, (c) *assay (=tries her mistress's lovers)*, I. I. 107.
score	*credit*, III. III. 19.
scowt	*deride*, PRO. 10.
Sectarie	*Protestant Dissenter*, III. IV. 113.
secure	*over-confident, unsuspecting*, II. I. 19.
securite	*culpable carelessness*, III. I. 215.
seet art	*sweetheart*, II. II. 48.
sencelesse	*without known explanation*, V. I. 79.
sentences	*sententiae*, II. II. 6.
service	*duty (with sexual innuendo)*, III. I. 188.
severe	*strict*, III. I. 45.
shamefastnes	*modesty*, II. I. 16.
Sharke	*Cheat* (cf. sharking, I. I. 43), I. I. 1.
sharpest	*harshest*, V. I. 57; *strictest*, V. I. 61.
Sha'te	*shall have it*, III. I. 3.
shaven	(a) *shaved*, (b) *stripped of possessions*, II. III. 23.
short heeles	*prostitute* (cf. chopines, III. I. 103), I. II. 93.
skonce	*head*, V. III. 71.
sincere	*exact, straightforward*, I. I. 14.
singled him	*took him to one side*, V. I. 44.
slidyngs	*backslidings, moral lapses*, II. I. 126.
soft	*pleasant, agreeable*, IV. I. 15.
somtimes	*sometime, former*, I. II. 87.
sounds	*swoons*, V. II. 38 S.D.
sowned	*swooned, fainted*, V. II. 39.
spurnd	*thrust with the foot*, or, *reject contemptuously*, V. I. 48.
stale	*decayed*, I. I. 96.
standing cup	*free-standing cup, chalice*, III. II. S.D.
still	*always, ever*, II. I. 39.
stocke	(a) *supply of liquor*, (b) *stocks*, IV. VII. 47.
stone-bowes	*(cross-) bow used for firing stones*, I. I. 24.
stoole	*privy*, I. II. 71.
straight	*at once*, IV. I. 18.
stranger	*foreigner*, IV. III. 37.
strong	*formidable*, IV. VII. 94.
studious	*diligent*, II. I. 63.
stuffe	*fabric (often of wool)*, IV. VII. 7.
suspitions	*suspicious circumstances, grounds of suspicion (now obsolete)*, V. II. 106.

swagger	*bluster*, II. II. I.
Synagogue	*Puritan name for a church*, III. IV. 112.
Syring	(a) *syringe*, (b) *penis*, I. II. 73.
tack	*join, "hitch" (in marriage)*, V. III. 149.
taking	(a) *state of arrest*, (b) *agitated state*, IV. VII. 72.
Tanakin	*diminutive of Anna, (used specifically for a German or Dutch girl)* (*O.E.D.*), I. I. 145.
tartar	*torture*, IV. III. 29.
taxe	*censure, condemn*, PRO. 12.
tentation	*temptation, trial*, II. II. 133.
then	*than, (passim).*
to	*too,* III. IV. 63; *compared to,* V. II. 15.
towards	*is in preparation,* III. IV. 16.
trat	*troth,* V. I. 22.
trim	(a) *shave,* (b) *cheat,* II. I. 195; *trimd:* II. III. 87, 88.
trot	*troth,* II. II. 63.
ubiquitari	*ubiquitous ones (i.e. whores),* IV. VI. 9.
uncaseth	*takes (his harp) out of its case,* I. I. 22.
uncollected	*unprepared,* II. II. 223.
unkind	*contrary to nature,* V. III. 101.
unnaturally	*indecorously, dishonestly,* I. I. 33.
unperegall	*unequalled,* IV. VII. 115.
use	*enjoy sexually,* III. I. 235.
venery	*sexual pursuits,* III. I. 27.
viah	*Come on! Away!,* I. II. 125.
vildest	*vilest,* IV. II. 37.
visitation	*visiting,* I. I. 53.
wagge	(a) *jester,* (b) *gossip,* III. I. 78.
Wagtaile	(a) *bird,* (b) *a loose woman (whose "tail" wags)* (cf. V. III. 4), IV. III. 6.
wa, ha, ho (*et sim.*)	*a falconer's cry* (cf. *M.o.V.* V. I. 39), (*passim*).
wanton	*merciless (rather than lascivious),* I. II. 135.
weake	*enfeebling,* V. II. 32.
Wenches	*wenchers* (*Wine*), V. I. 29.
whole sale	*antonym of retail (and also obscene pun),* I. II. 38.
whore of *Babylon*	*Roman Catholic Church (after Rev: 17.1, 15, 18),* V. III. 105.
winch	*wince, flinch,* III. IV. 13.
wished	*wished-for,* II. I. 61.
wit	*intellect,* II. II. 207.
worlds eye	*sun (and by implication "the eyes of all men"),* II. I. 124.
yout	*youth* (*Mock-Dutch*), II. II. 152.